IT'S ABOUT YOU TOO.

how to manage employee resistance to

your diversity initiatives and improve workplace culture and profitability

LORI B. RASSAS

Other Books by Lori B. Rassas

The Portable Perpetual Paycheck: Getting a Job, Keeping a Job, and Earning Income for Life in the Post-Pandemic Workplace

Negotiating Without the Nonsense: Straightforward and Effective Strategies to Obtain the Best Possible Compensation Package

Over the Hill but Not the Cliff: 5 Strategies for 50+ Job-Seekers to Push Past Ageism & Find a Job in the Loyalty-Free Workplace

The Perpetual Paycheck: 5 Secrets to Getting a Job, Keeping a Job, and Earning Income for Life in the Loyalty-Free Workplace (Volume 1)

The Perpetual Paycheck: 5 (More) Secrets to Getting a Job, Keeping a Job, and Earning Income for Life in the Loyalty-Free Workplace (Volume 2)

Employment Law: A Guide to Hiring, Firing, and Managing for Employers and Employees

DEDICATION

To my nieces Danica, Jamie, Logan, and Reese, and my nephew Davis,
none of whom resemble anyone in the cast of characters,
despite the fact that they may share the same name.

"You are never too young to change the world."
—Unknown

EPIGRAPHS

"Diversity includes everyone. Diversity excludes no one."
—2019 Federal Reserve Bank of Atlanta,
internal diversity and inclusion report

"The only thing we know about the future is that it will be different."
—Peter Drucker

"Strength lies in differences, not in similarities."
—Stephen Covey

TABLE OF CONTENTS

ACKNOWLEDGMENTS

I've always found writing a book to be hard work . . . but this one was especially challenging. I started it just as COVID-19 struck. I soon found myself writing while quarantining with various family members to avoid total isolation and minimize the risk of infection. From my writing bubble I witnessed the unprecedented divisiveness in our country: a historic presidential election, a divisive pandemic, and a national reckoning as we said the names of Breonna Taylor, George Floyd, Ahmaud Arbery, and so many others. Many of the central themes of the book were publicly contentious and sometimes acrimonious in professional circles. There were many (many) times when I contemplated tabling this book for a time or even adding it to my graveyard of failed writing ideas. But the more resistance I faced—real or just feared—the more committed I became to seeing the book through to its completion.

In my earlier books I've written of the need to go over, under, and through obstacles in order to reach your ultimate goals.[1] I decided to take my own advice. I realized the best way for me to make a significant impact on diversity issues was to push through the controversy and resistance. I knew I had an approach that could help managers across the country and across all industries deal with major issues they were facing.

As a trainer, the most common feedback I receive after delivering management workshops is, "Where have you been?" People often tell me mine was the first management training they'd received since becoming a manager, sometimes decades earlier. I'm not surprised by that since I've seen countless hiring managers laser focus on ensuring a candidate possesses all of the technical skills associated for a role and then, as an

---

1. I've included the chapter from my book *Over the Hill but Not the Cliff: 5 Strategies for 50+ Job-Seekers to Push Past Ageism & Find a Job in the Loyalty-Free Workplace* that makes this point as a bonus at the end of this book.

afterthought, advise the selected candidate, "By the way, you will also be managing a team of fifteen." I know that continuing to overlook management training has the potential to be even more problematic in our current climate.

Employers are investing significant resources to attract, recruit, and retain workforces that reflect the true diversity of our national and global workforce, but there are few, if any, resources being invested in teaching managers how to lead these diverse employees once they arrive. It's one thing to hire diverse employees. It's another thing to build and nurture those new workplace relationships to ensure they are meaningful and long-lasting, and produce the intended result.

I felt that recruiting a diverse workforce and then losing it due to poor management would leave an employer in a worse position than if they never took on the challenge in the first place. So, I decided to hunker down and commit to completing this project.

Even having made that decision, there was no way I could have completed this book without the unprecedented level of support and guidance I received from many people throughout the process. It has been incredibly humbling to have had countless people agree to help me navigate challenging conversations and respond to my never-ending requests for advice and feedback without hesitation.

First, I want to thank my family, who always unconditionally and wholeheartedly support me even before they (or even I) fully understand the scope of what lies ahead: my parents, Marge and Aaron; Stacey, Jeff, Logan, and Davis; Jessica, Eric, Danica, and Jamie; and Melissa, Jariel, and Reese. It is difficult for me to convey my gratitude in words . . . and you know that, coming from me, that says a lot. Stacey, Jeff, Logan, and Davis: I will be forever grateful for the fact that, less than two hours after I decided I wanted to tackle 2020 away from my permanent home, I had moved into your spare bedroom and was sitting at your kitchen table, where I became a consistent presence for many more months than any of us had anticipated. Logan and Davis: It has been a life-changing experience to see first-hand the two of you managing the trials and tribulations of the past year with an unwavering sense of optimism and, most importantly, such open and kind hearts. And I know when I first came to live with you, we worked to avoid "jumping the shark," but I truly enjoyed collectively letting go of that unattainable goal and doing the best we could based upon the circumstances we were in. Danica, Jamie, and Reese: You also have faced uncertain times in ways that are beyond your years and you also willingly opened your home to me. Danica and Jamie: When I first moved in with you and homeschooling began, I thought I might be able to help your parents teach you a few things. But, in fact, I was the one who learned an incredible amount from both of you.

I am also incredibly thankful to so many of my long-term friends and colleagues who offered me so much support and encouragement. While I could never provide a full list of the individuals who provided me guidance on so many levels, I do want to acknowledge a few close friends who went above and beyond: Marisol Abuin, Wade Baughman, Jen Biderman ("B"), Grace Brady, Donna Brown, Erin Cavanagh, Tina Fox, Rosemary Griffin, Felicia Hull, (Uncle) Harvey Jacob, Linda Lupiani, Marci, Jason, Harper, and Sloane Kroft, Ivy Lapides and Adam, Audrey, and Ezra Kolber, Keith Prewitt, Parisa Salehi, Tom Scally, Laura Scognamiglio, Ana Venegas, Mary Walsh, and Beth Wang. And a special thank you to my "high school" friends with whom I have been close for decades and whose friendships I value a great deal: Scott and Beth Atkins, Pam Brett, Jill Flynn, Kathleen Hassinger, Caroline Heyer, Chiara Kuhns, Christine Marosvary, and Tiffany Wysocki.

And I am especially grateful to Mark Levine: Thank you for guiding me through this entire book writing process. Your steady and masterful advice was instrumental in enabling me to convert the thoughts in my head into the clear and concise writing that fills the pages that follow. I am incredibly proud of the work that we have done as we navigated the world of differences, and I look forward to our continued collaborations.

I am confident that this final product will have a meaningful and immeasurable impact on any workplace that encourages and values those individuals who do not just tolerate or accept differences, but who readily embrace them.

A final note: As this book was making its way through the final level of review, I was already immersed in developing its successor, as well as a number of other instruments to make the process of working towards a more inclusive workplace more efficient and effective. One of the most important lessons writing this book has taught me is that the only way to truly establish an inclusive workforce is to accept that the effort is neither a sprint nor a marathon, but rather a never-ending process. Thank you for allowing me to be part of your journey.

— Lori B. Rassas, 2021

INTRODUCTION

UNCOMFORTABLE CONVERSATIONS

Let's have the uncomfortable conversations. The minute I decided to write a book about diversity, I knew I'd face criticism. I know the Diversity, Equity, Inclusion, and Accessibility (DEIA) space, and I know there are minefields. So, I'm humbled and appreciative of the fact that you've decided to give me a chance and at least read what I have to say.

I believe there is systemic racism in America. I believe working to overcome systemic racism is an important issue facing our country, especially in how it impacts health, economic, law enforcement, and political issues. I know that as a white woman who grew up middle class in suburbia, I have led a life of privilege.

It is *because* I believe these things, among others, that I'm suggesting efforts to expand the diversity of organizations must extend to considerations beyond legally protected classes and other characteristics that are most often discussed. I am a lawyer, and while I appreciate the legal focus on creating policies and procedures to protect an organization from legal liability, the focus of this book is somewhat different. And while I believe in the power of public pronouncements and visible signals of equity and inclusiveness, the focus of this book is something else. You see, I want to empower every single person with the tools and knowledge to make tangible and immediate changes that can impact businesses, institutions, and organizations of all sizes and across all industries. The fact that we are all different means we all share a common bond. The goal of this book is to turn as many people in your organization as possible into diversity advocates and allies for all of their coworkers.

In my experience, the best way to ensure that organizations become truly diverse, equitable, and inclusive, is for everyone to embrace diversity— from members of the leadership team, to the salespeople, to the production workers, to the administrative personnel. A truly diverse and inclusive culture can't be achieved by decree from the corner office. It won't happen because people at the grassroots wish it into existence. It will happen when everyone in the organization believes in it and sees it as worth the effort.

How do we do that? Time for our next uncomfortable conversation. I wish I could tell you that impassioned conversations and directives about creating a beloved community will convince your employees. Perhaps, over time, it will, but it hasn't yet. I don't know about you, but I don't have the patience to wait any longer. But I'm also not a revolutionary. I don't think tearing down an organization saves it any more than burning a village saves it. I think the answer is to do the best we can in the circumstances we are in.

I believe people are, perhaps not always but usually, motivated by self-interest. Certainly, the easiest and fastest way to influence people is to play to their self-interest. Anyone who spends any time trying to sell a product, a service, or an idea knows this. That's why I think that the best way to get your employees to accept and even promote diversity efforts is to show them that it benefits them personally. We have to illustrate that increased diversity benefits everyone in an organization collectively because it ensures the continued effectiveness and profitability of the organization in today's environment. And we also have to show them that increased diversity can benefit everyone in an organization individually. By expanding the idea of diversity to include more than just characteristics that are protected by federal, state, and local law, creating what I call the *diversity mosaic*, we give everyone a stake in an organization's diversity efforts.

In order to ensure organization-wide buy-in, we will need to expand our definition of the diversity mosaic to include the important traits protected by the most expansive state laws: ancestry, citizenship status, color, creed, domestic violence or stalking victim status, familial status, gender identity or expression, genetic information, marital status, medical conditions, military status, political activities or affiliation, predisposing genetic characteristics, pregnancy-related conditions, prior arrest or conviction record, unemployment status, retaliation for opposing unlawful discriminatory practices, service in the legislature, testimony in employment department hearings, union membership, use of a protected leave, and the use of tobacco products while off duty.

Then we need to expand our definition even further to include things that are not necessarily addressed by name legally, such as whether someone comes from poverty, the middle class, or affluence; whether they worked for one company for a long time or moved from job to job frequently; whether they have a college degree and, if so, whether it is a doctoral, master's, bachelor's or associate's; and whether they went to a community college, a state school, or an elite private university.

Finally, if we want to guarantee success, I believe we even need to include the less vital lifestyle aspects in our organization's diversity mosaic: what are the person's hobbies; are they an only child, or an older or younger sibling; are they renting, or do they own their own home; do they own a pet; and do they walk to work, drive from nearby, or take public transportation from quite a distance away. Each of these characteristics has an impact on how someone is treated at work and on their needs and wants and perception of the world.

Before I explain any further, let me stress again that not every element in the diversity mosaic is of equal importance. Obviously, it is more important that your organization is racially diverse than if it has employees who are both homeowners and renters. (Interestingly, however, many lifestyle and demographic issues tend to overlap with some of the more vital, legally protected characteristics.) The idea is to expand your diversity mosaic. Why? Because employees will be far less likely to object to a viewpoint or circumstance being acknowledged and considered if they know that their own viewpoint or circumstance will also be acknowledged and considered by the organization. And as employees become more and more accustomed to minority viewpoints being acknowledged and considered, they will move beyond acceptance and become allies of others who may be different from them in some way. The person who sees their problems with having a long commute addressed will stand with the person whose problems with caring for an elderly parent need to be addressed. And more importantly, the white employees will stand with the Black employees, the straight with the gay and transgender, the Christian with the Muslim, and so on.

I realize this is a process; it will not happen overnight. But it will happen.

My suggestion for speeding up this process requires another uncomfortable conversation. I believe that it is important for as many individuals as possible who represent minority viewpoints or circumstances be included in planning and decision-making to ensure a wide range of perspectives is considered. That sounds simple at first, but this asks of the individual who identifies with a minority viewpoint to become a "representative" for everyone else in that minority. In effect, they are sometimes treated as a spokesperson responsible for educating the rest of the group. It's one thing when that means someone is the only non-college graduate on the interview committee. But it's something else entirely when that means someone is the only person of color on that same committee. This can easily lead to resentment: *Why should I be responsible for educating the rest of the group? Why can't those people do it on their own? Why do I have to be the token on the committee?*

This sentiment is out there, and I get it.

In some ways, I agree, it may not be fair for an individual who has a particular characteristic to be the representative of all others who share it. I do not know anyone who embraces the idea of serving as the representative of all people of color, all disabled people, all lesbians, or, really, any other trait. And indeed, being the representative of some traits is less more troubling than others, e.g., having to represent all pet owners or all public transportation users. However, these voiced perspectives may be necessary in order to speed up the greater understanding of differences in our organizations.

I know it's not quite the same, but I once found myself in a situation where a group of individuals were about to schedule an event on Yom Kippur, the Jewish day of atonement, which mandates day-long prayer and fasting. As a Jewish person who observes this holiday, I had to point out that I didn't think that was a good idea. To their credit, the group immediately understood and felt a bit embarrassed by their lack of knowledge and awareness. But for a number of discussions in the following year, I became the go-to resource for all things Jewish: they turned to me for the "Jewish perspective" on holidays and menus. I thought, *I'm not a rabbi. I'm not even Orthodox.*[2] *Why do I have to be the representative of all Jews? Why can't the group just Google Jewish holidays and Kosher dietary laws?*

I found this experience to be uncomfortable, and while I understand the group was reaching out to me to be sure I and other Jewish stakeholders felt included, in many ways it made me feel more excluded than I might have been had some missteps actually happened. I can imagine how, in a similar situation, someone who is "selected" as the go-to person of color, for example, would have experienced a different expanse and range of emotions than I did.

Please do not misinterpret what I am saying here. I am *not* saying you should agree to hours upon hours of unpaid or emotionally taxing work because you are the only person in your workplace who has a particular characteristic, or because you feel pressured to represent everyone who shares a particular characteristic with you, or because you get the feeling if you do not do it, no one else will. And I am *not* saying you should blindly agree to generously share all of your personal experiences and any knowledge you have about a particular characteristic you have that is noticeably underrepresented. However, I *am* saying you should be willing to presume good intent, share any information you have at your fingertips, and be willing to hear out anyone with an interest in learning more about your "diversity mosaic" characteristics, perhaps providing guidance as to where they should go to learn more. And you might be surprised to find that just inching this door ajar *without* opening the floodgates might result in you learning new information and establishing a new connection that brings true value to you and the pursuit of your goals. Responding positively, rather than with a heated response denouncing your role as the representative of everyone who happens to share one of your characteristics, will bring us all closer to greater acceptance for all of our differences.

---

2. One of the three major branches of Judaism that advocates a strict observance of Jewish law.

Yes, it is true that my organization should have known better than to schedule an event on Yom Kippur and could have, and perhaps should have, expended the effort necessary to learn information about this holiday as well as other holidays and related traditions on their own. I could have spared myself the discomfort and not spoken up, and the group would likely have received criticism for scheduling an event on the holiest day of the Jewish year. But my willingness to provide context for the decision to a well-meaning but uninformed group prevented them from being subject to that criticism. I felt, and still feel, that it was worth it. It may not have been fair, and it may have singled me out in a way I did not fully embrace, but it helped speed up reaching the goal of an equitable and inclusive organization.

Now, for one more uncomfortable conversation. One of the reasons I volunteered information to the group about Jewish traditions and customs was that I knew my team was a well-meaning group of people who wanted to do the right thing. I think that this belief, the belief that most people mean well and want to do what is right, is vital to making our organizations more equitable and inclusive.

Sometimes people say and do things that are biased, ignorant, discriminatory, and hurtful. And because organizations are comprised of individuals with a wide range of perspectives, organizations can also be biased, ignorant, discriminatory, and hurtful. Years, decades, and even generations of people experiencing bias, ignorance, discrimination, and pain make it understandable for those who are victimized to assume ill intentions on the part of others.

However, I refuse to believe that everyone who exhibits these beliefs or actions are intentionally malicious. I believe some may not know any better and that their beliefs and actions may be the result of a narrow upbringing or life experience. Yes, there are immoral people out there, but they are few and far between. I don't think we should live our lives assuming others are evil or intentionally seek to cause harm or discomfort. If we do, we close ourselves off from the good in the world, allowing cynicism and pessimism to rule our lives. We risk becoming what we are fighting against.

What I am sure of is that it is better to assume that others mean well and want to do the right thing. Let's have the uncomfortable conversations. Let's reach out to our coworkers with an open mind and an open heart. Let's commit to working tirelessly together to implement real changes that will benefit everyone. To do that, we'll need the right tools. I hope this book can be one of them.

CHAPTER 1
THE DIVERSITY MOSAIC

Let's play a quick word association game. What's the first word or phrase that comes to mind when I say "diversity"? Don't be embarrassed. Whenever I play this game with a group of employees, almost everyone immediately says "race." If I press for more responses, people will mention "gender" and "sexual orientation." "Ethnicity" and "religion" will be cited. Often, if there are people over age 40 in the group, one of them will say "age." If someone in the group has a disability or has a disabled family member or friend, they'll offer the word "disability."

These seven terms immediately come to people's minds because their perception of diversity is that it's all about ensuring an organization doesn't violate the rights of individuals who belong to the categories protected by employment laws. I believe this narrow understanding of what diversity means is a major reason why people don't become instant and enthusiastic supporters of diversity mosaic efforts. They'll say they're supportive, but those hidden thought bubbles tell another story. Whatever the cause, they're harboring doubts and fears about attitudes, behaviors, approaches, and appearances different from their own.

How do you think people would feel about diversity efforts if the first seven words or phrases that came to mind were "working parent," "train commuter," "union member," "middle income," "veteran," "college graduate," and "homeowner," some of which might apply to themselves? We'd see lots of those hidden thought bubbles show immediate and whole-hearted support for diversity mosaic efforts.

I'm not trying to minimize the importance of overcoming workplace bias based on race, gender, sexual orientation, ethnicity, religion, age, or disability. I'm also not suggesting that having an organization in which people commute to work by different means is as important as having an organization that is racially diverse. I am suggesting that if your goal is to expand the diversity of your organization, the best way to do that is to have your employees become advocates of the effort. And the best way to turn employees into advocates is to frame the effort as one that will definitely benefit them and will potentially benefit others.

WE SUBCONSCIOUSLY DIVIDE THE WORLD INTO "US" AND "THEM."

As painful as it is to admit, everyone subconsciously divides the world into "us" and "them." Hundreds of psychological tests have shown that there is something deep within us that drives us to view differences as bad, and that this drive may even be innate to humans. That's where the psychological agreement ends, however.

Some psychologists believe that we look to boost our self-esteem by being part of distinct and elite groups, playing up the qualities of our own "in-group" and downplaying the qualities of other "out-groups." This social identity theory suggests that the way we categorize these groups doesn't necessarily have to do with the typical divisions we associate with bias—traits such as race, national origin, or religion. Instead, we can divide people by any criteria. Those who are fans of the New York Yankees may consider themselves an "in-group" and the fans of the Boston Red Sox an "out-group." People who attend or have graduated from Ivy League universities may see themselves as an "in-group," better than the "out-group" from state universities. Experiments have shown that people can divide the world this way using even the most minor characteristics. One well-known experiment had a classroom of third graders divide themselves into those who had blue eyes and those who had brown or green eyes, resulting in discord.

Another theory suggests that we are uncomfortable with differences because early in our evolution, those who shared traits with us were biologically related to us. In this theory, we divide the world into those who are genetically close to us and those who are not, and by favoring those who are close to us, we help perpetuate our genes. As we evolved, we simply began applying this same kind of bias to more and more traits that had no genetic link.

Finally, we may be uncomfortable with differences due to implicit biases. Our implicit biases are activated involuntarily, without our awareness or control, and may materialize into a positive or negative attitude toward a group of people or characteristic. To provide some context, in his book *Blink*, Malcolm Gladwell refers to our conscious biases as what we choose to believe and our implicit or unconscious biases as the immediate, automatic associations that tumble out before we've had time to think.

These biases develop throughout our lives, through exposure to direct and indirect messages that we start to receive from a young age. These messages come from a range of sources such as television, movies, books, family, friends, and social interactions. This means we all have different implicit biases based upon the composition of our families, our economic status, the area we grow up in, the faith communities in which we are raised, the schools we attend, the media we are exposed to, and the movies and other entertainment we consume. These implicit biases are prevalent in our day-to-day interactions because they serve as shortcuts. Rather than having to take the time to weigh the pros and cons and make reasoned judgments, we might just make a reflexive decision based on an implicit bias.

These biases may surface in a number of different contexts. For example, the correspondence bias is the tendency to believe that someone's actions correspond with who they are at their core. How does this materialize? We jump to the conclusion that someone who cuts into the line at the baggage check is selfish and rude, without taking the time to consider that this is not their usual behavior and finding out they are doing it now only because they are late for a flight to visit a dying relative. Confirmation bias is the tendency to be biased toward things that confirm our preexisting beliefs for values. If you already believe people who live in rural areas are less educated, you may instinctively view the otherwise neutral activities or behaviors of rural residents as confirming your preexisting belief. The beauty bias is the tendency to be positively biased toward people whom you find attractive. One well-known experiment had an attractive woman ask for help from bystanders in stealing a bicycle. Individuals were more likely to believe the woman's far-fetched explanation and help her steal the bike than they were to help an average-looking person in the exact same situation.

Whatever the reason, it's critical to recognize that your employees may have both conscious and subconscious uneasiness about anyone, any approach, or anything that is different to them. Because of this, we have to be aware and be prepared to address their discomfort.

DIVERSITY OF PERSPECTIVE IS THE ESSENTIAL FEATURE OF A SUCCESSFUL 21ST-CENTURY ORGANIZATION.

From a societal perspective, these explicit and implicit attitudes about differences have potential personal and political implications. From a business perspective, which is the viewpoint of this book, discomfort or uneasiness, in whatever form, has a significant and definable impact on the current and future health and success of organizations. The very things your employees are consciously or reflexively uncomfortable with—differences—are also the most essential ingredients for your organization's success.

A great deal has been written about how America is becoming more racially and ethnically diverse. According to recent Census Bureau estimates, non-Hispanic whites made up about 63% of the U.S. population; Hispanics and Latinos of any race about 15%; Black or African Americans about 13%; Asians about 6%; people identifying as being two or more races about 3%; Native Americans and Alaska Natives about 1%; and Native Hawaiians and Other Pacific Islanders about 0.2%. By 2050, again according to Census Bureau projections, non-Hispanic whites will make up about 46% of the U.S. population; Hispanics and Latinos of any race about 30%; Black or African Americans about 15%; Asians about 9%; people identifying as being two or more races about 9%; Native Americans and Alaska Natives about 2%; and Native Hawaiians and Other Pacific Islanders about 0.4%. (For a graphic look at these numbers, take a look at the charts on page 13 and compare the sizes of the pie slices.) The Census Bureau projects that the United States will become a minority-majority nation, with less than 50 percent of the population self-identifying as non-Hispanic, single-race whites, by 2042.

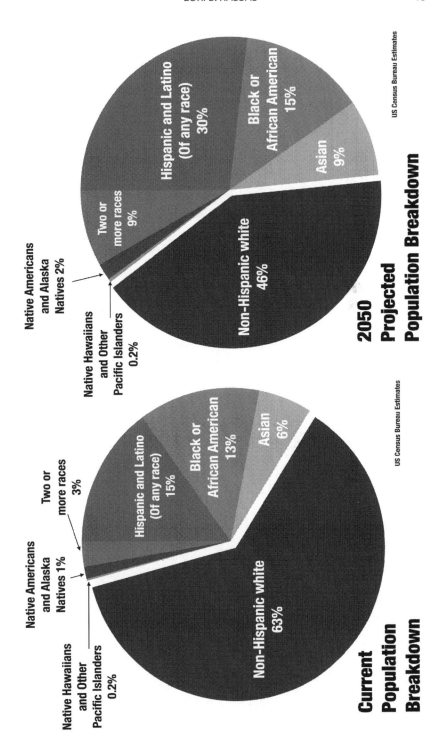

Current
Population
Breakdown

2050
Projected
Population Breakdown

US Census Bureau Estimates

The working population, which the Census Bureau categorizes as those between the ages of 18 and 64, will become minority-majority by 2039. Many demographers predict those tipping points will come even sooner.

For better or worse, these racial and ethnic trends receive most of the attention when people think of how the United States is changing. But they don't tell the whole story. For example, cohabitation, as opposed to marriage, is on the rise as younger adults delay marriage. That doesn't necessarily mean they are delaying parenthood; increasing numbers of children are living with an unmarried parent. The United States now has the world's highest rate of children living in single-parent households. The millennial generation consists of a greater percentage of college graduates than prior generations, but they're buying homes at a much lower rate. Suburban areas and small cities are growing faster than urban counties, which in turn are growing faster than rural areas. The foreign-born share of the population is increasing. The percentage of the population who identify as Christian is shrinking, while the percentages of those who identify as unaffiliated with any religion, or affiliated with non-Christian religions are growing. The percentage of disabled individuals in the workplace is increasing. Fewer people are driving to work alone. More people are working from home than ever, and that was even before the shift to remote work due to the coronavirus pandemic. I could go on, but the point I'm making is that we are moving further and further from the cookie-cutter world of the early 20th century in many different ways.

When we talk about differences, we're talking about far more than race, ethnicity, religion, gender, sexual orientation, national origin, age, or disability. The differences your business needs to embrace become a mosaic of lifestyle and demographic factors. America is becoming a more multifaceted society in which organizations' constituents represent an ever-increasing number of different perspectives. To anticipate and address all these different perspectives, organizations need to be as diverse as the society in which they operate. Understanding and adapting to this diversity mosaic is now essential for any organization to survive and thrive. And this means it will become critical for employees to be on board with the idea as well.

Workplace diversity will be the key feature of every successful 21st century organization, as it ensures the organization is empathetic to the needs of *all* of its constituents and empowers *all* of its employees to advance professionally and personally. It provides the organization with the insights and creativity to be innovative and adaptable in today's ever-changing environment. And it helps build the kind of visionary, inclusive culture needed to be profitable now and in the future.

I also believe that to do that, you need to change the results of the word association game we played at the beginning of this chapter. You need to expand the concept of diversity to include more than just the legally protected classes, showing that it provides important business advantages, not just legal defense. You need to show that diversity refers to the traits of everyone. These characteristics should not divide us; instead, they should bring us together. You need to change employees' perceptions of diversity from concerning how others might hurt the organization, by perhaps a lawsuit or the threat of a lawsuit, to that which concerns them and the organization's future success. You need to create an organization in which employees feel that every other employee is an ally, not an opponent, however different their mosaic of traits might be.

* * *

Employers first began looking at the demographics of their employees in response to legislation intended to put an end to various forms of workplace discrimination. Awareness of the discrimination faced by various categories of individuals gradually expanded the types of characteristics that fell under the protective umbrella of federal, state, and local legislation. All of this legislation was written to provide remedies for those who have been discriminated against. The laws provided negative reinforcement: if you don't expand the diversity of your workforce, you will be legally liable for damages from employees who prove discrimination.

Creating protected classes divided employees into those who were covered and those who were not. It turned workplace diversity into a tense "us-versus-them" issue, involving lawsuits with winners and losers. Diversity efforts could lead to job loss and financial ruin for individuals who "lost." For the company, winning or losing the lawsuit sometimes didn't even matter—either way, it meant legal fees, lowered morale, bad publicity, and even boycotts if that publicity became viral.

The existence of protected classes can be read by some as implying that there is something wrong with members of those classes. How? Well, if you're a hiring manager and are told that you're not permitted to consider a candidate's age when making a decision, you might assume that if you could consider it, it would be the basis for a rejection.

Efforts to preemptively keep hiring managers from doing something wrong presumes bad intent on that person's part. It says to managers that they're not trusted to know the difference between right and wrong. No one needs to tell a manager that they can't steal another person's car from the parking lot. The company doesn't assume all its employees are natural car thieves who must be explicitly told not to commit auto theft.

Protected classes create the impression of exclusivity: certain people get benefits that others do not. For example, those who identify with a religion are in a protected class, while those who do not identify with a religion are not.

Finally, the creation of protected classes has the potential to take one characteristic of an employee and make it the central element of their identity. For example, Ali becomes "the Muslim employee," not the "Excel wizard," homeowner, married father of two, or speaker of four languages. Employees who aren't Muslim may not see Ali's other traits, some of which they might share.

This division of people into narrowly drawn categories has resulted in people who don't fall into one of the classes viewing diversity efforts as protecting "others," not them. It's no wonder that many employees have doubts and fears about diversity efforts when they see those efforts as protecting the company against the *potential* actions of "*others*" who are defined solely by the trait that gives them membership in a protected class.

WE ARE MORE THAN JUST ONE TRAIT.

Intersectionality is an approach to social identity coined by feminist scholar Kimberlé Crenshaw in the late 1980s, building on ideas from sociologist W. E. B. Du Bois in the early 20th century and activist and feminist Sojourner Truth in the mid-19th century. The idea behind it is that a single characteristic cannot be viewed as the only factor in someone having advantages or disadvantages as compared to others. The idea is that a Black woman doesn't face discrimination solely because she is Black or solely because she is a woman; instead she faces discrimination due to the intersection of the two characteristics. Similarly, a straight white man doesn't have privilege solely because he is male or solely because he is straight, but because of the intersection of the two characteristics. The importance of intersectionality when it comes to getting people to buy into and advocate for diversity mosaic efforts is that it provides the intellectual foundation for the concept that everyone is more than just a single characteristic, regardless of whether that characteristic places someone in a protected class or not.

Rather than characterize people using a single characteristic, you need to explain to employees that they—and the company—should view everyone, including themselves, as a unique mosaic of dozens of different characteristics. Certainly, characteristics under the umbrella of protected classes are part of the mosaics of everyone who fits into them.

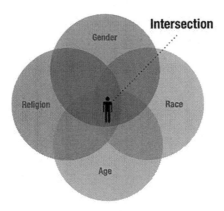

Yes, your race, gender, ethnicity, sexual orientation, religion, national origin, and age are important. But you're much more than just those characteristics.

Do you define yourself politically as a conservative Republican, a progressive Democrat, a moderate Independent, or do you identify with another party?

Have you served in the military?

Are you married or single?

Do you have children?

Are you pregnant?

Have you ever been arrested?

Which languages do you speak?

Are you currently employed?

Would you say that you come from an impoverished, middle-income, or affluent background? Which of those economic levels would you say you currently fit into?

Do you belong to a union?

Have you worked for one company for a long time, or do you have a history of hopping from job to job frequently?

Do you have a college degree? Is it an associate's, a bachelor's, a master's, or a doctorate?

Did you go to a community college, an elite private college, or a state university?

Do you like to watch sports, knit, hike, do woodworking, bake, play an instrument, paint, or dance?

Are you an only child, the firstborn, or the youngest of your siblings?

Are you caring for an elderly parent or a special needs child?

Are you renting or do you own your own home?

Do you live in the city, the suburbs, or a rural area?

Do you own a pet?

Do you walk to work, drive from nearby, or take public transportation from quite a distance away?

Each of these characteristics—and dozens I haven't named—has an impact on how you are treated as well as your needs, your wants, and your perception of the world, just as every protected characteristic has an impact. It's not a question of ranking characteristics by significance—it's obvious that some are more important than others. The point is that they all have some impact on perceptions. Someone caring for an elderly parent, for example, may view the organization's family leave policy differently from someone who has school-age children. As you'll see in the following chapters, having access to a wide a range of points of view is essential to your organization's success.

Your goal is to get people to stop looking at themselves through the prism of protected classes and instead view everyone as a unique mosaic of dozens of different characteristics. Take a look at the two diagrams on page 20. When employees look at themselves, they need to move from the image on the left to the image on the right.

Don't believe that each of these characteristics could be important or provide a different perspective? Let's take a look at a couple of situations.

You are sitting in an exclusive, five-star restaurant, having a late dinner with a friend. It's an evening you've been looking forward to. A family is soon seated at a nearby table. There are two adults and two very young children. The children are so young, the hour so late, and the restaurant so expensive that you're surprised by their presence. Clearly, so is the staff, who explain to the parents that they don't have a highchair for the youngest. You turn to the person you're dining with and express your surprise. How do they react?

That probably depends on whether they possess some of those characteristics I've mentioned.

Is your dining partner a parent? If your dining partner has children of their own, they could be sympathetic to the parents at the next table's situation. Your dining partner might comment that those parents might not have had a night out in months and that their babysitting plans probably fell through.

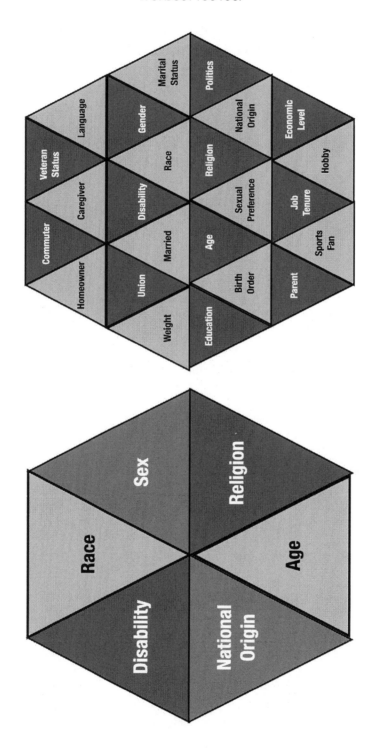

If your dining partner doesn't have children, they could be annoyed at the parents and criticize them for bringing young children to the restaurant which might disrupt the dining experience you and your friend were looking forward to. Your child-free partner might even criticize the parents at the other table for being selfish.

If your dining partner is affluent enough to go out to fine restaurants regularly, they might not be concerned since this dinner isn't a rarity for them. A judgmental dining partner might wonder what responsible adult would have a child out of the house at such a late hour.

On the other hand, if your dining partner lives on a fixed income and rarely gets to go out to fine restaurants, they could be very worried that this once-a-year event will be spoiled by those young children at the next table.

Let's look at another situation, this time in the workplace.

The organization has just won a big new contract. To celebrate, the CEO proposes taking everyone on the team out for dinner on Friday night after work. Elizabeth, who lives near the office and walks to work, thinks this is a great idea. Jabar, who lives about thirty minutes from the office and drives to and from work, has mixed feelings. Sakura, who lives an hour from the office and takes a suburban commuter train, thinks it's a terrible idea. Something you'd think would be an innocuous characteristic—the details of someone's daily commute—has a big impact on how they perceive a situation, while the facts that Elizabeth has a disability, Jabar is gay, and Sakura is Japanese-American have nothing to do with how they feel about the plan.

Now, let's consider some different scenarios that illustrate how a combination of characteristics could make perceptions even more complex. Elizabeth, Jabar, and Sakura together form the recruiting committee to help fill an open position in the organization. Elizabeth has a bachelor's degree from an Ivy League university and has held four different jobs in the past five years. Jabar has a master's degree from a state university and has had three jobs in the past ten years. Sakura has worked for the organization for more than twenty years, having been hired right after leaving the military; the organization paid for Sakura's tuition while she earned an associate's degree at the local community college two years ago.

This committee is reviewing three finalists for the open position and are having a hard time agreeing.

The first candidate has a master's degree from a prestigious university and has worked at five different jobs in the past five years. Elizabeth and Jabar are impressed by the candidate's education, but Sakura is concerned with the candidate's job-hopping.

The second has a bachelor's degree from a state university and has held three jobs since leaving the military ten years ago. Elizabeth and Jabar have mixed feelings about the candidate's education, while Sakura is impressed by their military service.

The third has an associate's degree and has worked for the same company for five years. Sakura is impressed by the candidate's long tenure, while Elizabeth and Jabar express some concerns over their education.

If only one of the candidates was a baseball fan like Elizabeth and Sakura—a seemingly arbitrary characteristic—that could have made them first choice.

I shouldn't be flippant. But I'm trying to convey that every characteristic, no matter how irrelevant it may seem, can have some impact on perceptions. And since every one of us has multiple characteristics, even those that seem inconsequential can contribute to our overall perception of an individual, an approach, a product, a process, or a situation. That's exactly what you need to convey to your employees and peers.

They're going to think it takes a great deal of effort to be cognizant of creating as diverse an employee mosaic as possible. They're right. It *would* be so much easier if everyone were just like them. If single people without children went to restaurants that only allowed others without children, they'd never have to worry about young children potentially spoiling the atmosphere of their expensive dinners. And if their company only hired people who graduated from Ivy League universities, hiring decisions *would* be a lot easier. But the effort involved in helping build a diverse employee mosaic will be a drop in the bucket compared to the benefits the organization will derive from having all those different perspectives in the workforce.

It's vital that your staff understands that having as diverse a population in your organization as possible, representing as many different characteristics as possible—not just protected classes—gives your organization the broadest possible perspective when making business decisions. A broad perspective helps in making sound and fair hiring choices; developing effective marketing, recruiting, and advertising programs; managing and empowering employees; and thoughtfully analyzing strategic opportunities. The good news is that even though your employees' fears and concerns about differences may be deep-seated, they can be overcome. Employees can be brought along to see that differences are vital for the organization's future success and their personal discomfort may be due to correctable management mistakes, such as neglecting to address the potential frustrations of employees with children, or perhaps their own subconscious misapprehensions. Either way, once there is an understanding of the reason for the discomfort, resistance disappears. Once they're brought along, employees who once might have opposed efforts to expand the diversity of your organization will accept the importance of adding new perspectives and become advocates for diversity mosaic efforts.

The purpose of this book is to help you bring others along in your personal efforts to expand the diversity mosaic of your organization—whether it's the five staffers working in the gift shop you own, the dozen team managers you oversee as director of operations of a nonprofit, or your ten peers on the leadership team of the business whose CEO has tasked you with implementing a DEIA plan. I will give you the strategies to solve these issues and turn reluctant and ambivalent employees into advocates of your diversity efforts.

But there's more to it than that. Becoming a diverse organization means achieving a demographic mix of human differences including, but not limited to, historically underrepresented and marginalized groups. Once you have a diverse group of individuals under your workplace umbrella, you need to do all that you can to make your organization as inclusive as it is diverse, ensuring that underrepresented groups participate in decision-making.

When people in an organization who are not members of a protected group accept the concept of the diversity mosaic, they will gain personally as well. Understanding that there are various perspectives can lead people to lose some self-centered attitudes and behaviors about the world, not just their workplace. A broader view of the world can lead to a wider social network, breaking down artificial interpersonal silos. The more the "us versus them" worldview eases, the more confident and empowered people will become.

This isn't mission impossible. I'm not saying it will be easy to change your organization, but I've done it and so can you. However, like those impossible missions, this one can't be done through conventional means. The greatest mistake of most efforts to expand the diversity of organizations has been to approach it as a legal project focused solely on issues such as race, religion, gender, sexual orientation, age, or disability. If your method of motivation is the predictable approach— "we need to do this to avoid the threat of legal action"—the most you'll ever achieve is grudging acceptance. Grudging acceptance might be enough to keep lawsuits at bay— and I'll tell you all about the legal issues in a later chapter—but it's not enough to maintain your organization's morale or retain top talent. And it's far from enough to set up your organization for long-term success. Grudges will lead to cracks in your organization. The increased diversity of American society is as inevitable as the rising tides, and it involves far more than just legally protected classes of people. Fight against the tide and you and your organization will not survive. Choose to tread water and you'll stay afloat until your strength eventually runs out ... and then the organization will sink along with you. But if you keep your team together and learn to ride the wave, your organization will be in position to grow and prosper in a changing society. In the following chapters, I am going to tell you precisely how to accomplish just this.

TAKEAWAYS

- The common perception is that diversity efforts are all about ensuring an organization doesn't violate the rights of individuals who belong to the categories protected by employment laws.
- To turn all employees into advocates of diversity efforts, the efforts need to be framed as benefitting them as well as everyone else in the organization, not just those who belong to protected classes.
- People subconsciously divide the world into "us" and "them."

- This approach might be done to boost our self-esteem by being part of distinct and elite groups.
- Our implicit biases lead us to make decisions and judgments on subconscious associations rather than facts or even our true feelings.
- Differences in perspective is the essential feature of a successful 21st century organization.
- The differences your organization needs to embrace are a mosaic of lifestyle and demographic factors.
- You need to expand the concept of diversity to include more than just protected categories and show that it provides important business defenses and advantages, not just a legal defense.
- You need to change employees' perception of diversity from being about others who might hurt the organization to being about them and the organization's future success.
- Intersectionality provides the foundation for the concept that everyone is more than just a single characteristic.
- Every characteristic has an impact on how someone is treated as well as their needs, wants, and perceptions of the world.

CHAPTER 2
TRUTH VISION AND THE
CAST OF CHARACTERS

Senior leaders in organizations across the country are having uncomfortable conversations about diversity issues. Throughout this book we'll navigate these issues from the perspective of a hypothetical CEO and COO and watch how they deal with these discussions. Ironically, the most difficult exchanges often begin innocuously. . . .

"But we've always served ham at the Christmas party."

"I know that, Eric, but with all our recent hires we don't think it sends the right message."

Even before Eric's comment, Angel Rodriguez, the COO, was dreading leading the discussion about the company's annual holiday party with the leadership team at their weekly meeting. But he couldn't put it off any longer because Shanelle Lapides, the CEO, had been pressing him about it.

As the discussion progresses, it seems organizing this party is as complex and fraught with challenges as arranging a state dinner at the White House.

"Do we need to have the party during work hours? It's so much more festive to have it after work," says Asa.

"I understand that, Asa," Angel replies, "but the unionized staff would need to be paid for that time and the budget just won't cover it. Am I right about that, Jabar?"

"You are. Besides, some of us have a long trip home and don't want to be getting home late."

"And any single parents would need to arrange for childcare," adds Jessenia. "It's not fair that they would have that added expense."

"Hey, I had to pick up the slack for all the parents on staff lots of times during the pandemic, and you didn't hear me complaining," Max explains.

"Well, complaining is what you're doing now," Logan snaps back.

"Complaints are what we're going to hear from Sam at Reception and Sharon in Security if we have the party during work hours and they're not able to attend," warns Stacey.

Amy grins and is about to say something, when Angel jumps in.

"Okay, let's not start bickering," Angel says, trying to forestall a free-for-all. "I'm going to go back to Shanelle and get some input on the plan."

"Good idea," notes Aaron. "This really isn't an issue we should be responsible for. Let's move on to the next item."

* * *

One week later

"Here's the update on the staff party," Angel announces with more confidence than he feels. "Shanelle and I had a long discussion. It's been decided that there will be no party. Instead, Shanelle's going to take the money that would have been spent on the party and divide it equally among everyone in the company as a special end-of-year bonus. There will also be no Christmas tree in the lobby like there has been in the past."

"Just another example of the war on Christmas," Amy barks.

Angel was expecting this.

"No, Amy. It's just that the boss doesn't want a repeat of issues the like we had last year."

"I still don't get it," Amy responds with a smirk. "All I did was try to spread some holiday cheer by wishing Mordechai and Mohammed a merry Christmas during our holiday toast."

"Yes, Amy, we all remember," says Angel.

* * *

Situations like these are common in today's workplaces. Employees are no different than anyone else: they have doubts and concerns about people, attitudes, and approaches that are different from those they've dealt with, what they've thought, and what they've experienced in the past. People don't reflexively embrace change and differences.

The solution that Angel and Shanelle came up with may work, but it's a blunt, short-term fix. They just threw up their hands and looked for the easiest way out of the mess that the holiday party had become. That's understandable. Most of us would do the same the first time we were faced with this type of conflict. But things don't need to be that way. Managing the various qualms and fears employees have about the diversity mosaic efforts of an organization can present opportunities rather than crises. They are opportunities to improve morale and workplace culture, and position the organization to protect itself against mistakes and seize new opportunities in today's workplace and business environment.

The characters we met in this hypothetical scenario about the organization's holiday party are open about their feelings because they're part of a tight executive team and know their weekly leadership meeting is a safe place where they can say whatever they think and feel without repercussions. You may not realize how common thoughts like those of the characters are among your own employees because many employees think they should keep their anxieties about differences to themselves.

Most employees won't want to say anything that could even remotely be perceived as biased in today's vigilant environment. So, few people will feel free to voice their dismay about how religious needs may impact their organization, as Eric did. And almost no one would give voice to outright discrimination, as Amy did.

However, it's not just feelings about protected classes of people that your employees might not want to talk about. Every demographic and lifestyle element of the diversity mosaic represents a difference that can make employees feel awkward, but they might not be comfortable voicing that discomfort.

Single parents might not want to bring up the added burdens they face because they don't want to hurt their future career opportunities. And childfree employees like Max probably won't be inclined to speak up about their frustrations at not getting the same kind of attention and support as employees who have children, because it could make them appear callous and unsupportive.

Perhaps someone has a dietary concern related to a health issue (rather than a religious need) that they don't want to raise out of privacy concerns. (*No one needs to know I have irritable bowel syndrome.*) Someone might feel that unionized employees are low on the totem pole, and so their needs shouldn't impact everyone else, but might not want to advertise their elitism. (*We can easily replace the security guards so we shouldn't have to accommodate them.*) Someone who lives within walking distance of the office may not want to say anything about people who leave early because of a long commute. (*If I advertise that I walk to the office, I could be the one who's always asked to come in for emergencies.*)

Your first step in expanding the diversity of your organization is to understand the unspoken as well as spoken feelings of the employees you need to bring along. Identifying and understanding the feelings held by the employees at every level of your organization regarding attitudes, behaviors, approaches, and appearances that are different from what they have experienced in the past can take huge investments of time and money. You can bring in an outside team of expensive consultants and have them conduct in-depth interviews and focus groups with people throughout your organization, probing for hidden resistance and its root causes. You can create an ad hoc team of in-house leaders and have them spend a great deal of their time for the next six months brainstorming. Or you can borrow my superpower.

I HAVE TRUTH VISION.

I can see the thought bubbles above the heads of the people in your organization. I know what they're thinking even as they appear to be grateful for a member of the planning committee bringing up yet another point. I know the objections they're going to be voicing amongst one another when the boss isn't in the room. I know the fears they're going to be sharing in private conversations with their workplace buddies and personal texts with their family. I even know some of the thoughts they will never say out loud. It wasn't gamma rays that gave me this super-power—it was years of working with employers and employees at all levels and in a wide range of industries as they navigated the hiring and firing processes. Those conversations occurred in both group and private meetings and were often followed by the coaching of individuals and teams.

I know the people you're working with. Although every organization is unique, every level in every organization does have a similar cast of characters. These are workplace archetypes that populate the tech staff of a small software start-up, the teachers in a suburban middle school, and the directors of a multimillion-dollar business. You'll recognize these people as individuals you're working with now or worked with in the past. You might also recognize some of these character traits in people with whom you have personal relationships. And with some true self-reflection, you may even recognize some of these characteristics in yourself.

I've tried to have some fun in the naming and descriptions of these characters. Please understand that I think all these characters are basically good people. They, like everyone, are composites of their upbringing and past experiences at home and at work. I have found that most people are good, want to work hard, and want their organization to succeed. They only need guidance to help them overcome any unjustified fears or concerns about differences they might harbor, either consciously or subconsciously.

With that said, let's look at the people who are populating your organization. You already met some of them in the beginning of the chapter when they were discussing the hypothetical holiday party. We'll get into specifics later in the book, but for now, let's look at what, in general, they are thinking about diversity mosaic efforts, and start thinking about how to manage each of them.

Name		Motto
Shanelle Lapides CEO		"Make it work!"
Angel Rodriguez COO		"How do I make it work?"
Jabar Pyncher *The Penny Pincher*		"What's the ROI?"
Stacey MacArthur *The General*		"How is this relevant?"
Eric Luddy *The Enemy of Change*		"Don't fix what's not broken."
Bea Crawford *The Narcissist*		"How will this impact me?"
Aaron Brady *The Buck Passer*		"This has nothing to do with me or my team."
Jessenia Cannon *The Projector*		"I'm supportive, but how will others react?"
Theresa Stewart *The Saint*		"My team is perfect."
Jamie Little *The Alarmist*		"What if…?"
Max Yorkshire *The One-Upman*		"No one did that for me."
Waylon Jones *The Brown-Noser*		"Great idea, boss!"
Mai Olaf *The Pollyanna*		"Let's look on the bright side."
Davis Orr *The Defender*		"I don't think there's a problem."
Reese Geller *The Control Freak*		"I've already taken care of it."
Carlos Brownsky *The Victim*		"But what about my problem?"
Danika Casper *The Wallflower*		"…"
Asa Lattery *The Procrastinator*		"I'll get to it."
Logan Brita *The Tactless*		"I tell it like it is."
Amy Bunker *The Lawsuit*		"Don't be so PC."

Shanelle Lapides, CEO

When Shanelle Lapides was made CEO, the board made it clear they were looking for her to bring the organization into the 21st century. The prior CEO was beloved, but the board felt he'd been resting on his laurels for a while and the organization was stagnating as a result. Shanelle's reputation is that of a strategic thinker, a visionary who focuses on the big picture. Decisive to a fault, Shanelle is open to all points of view and arguments, but after she hears everyone out, she makes a decision and moves on. She is known to focus on the long term and external issues, and believes in delegating responsibility for operational issues.

"Tell me what resources and tools you need and I'll get them for you, but then I expect you to deliver," was the message she gave to her leadership team at their first meeting.

Angel Rodriguez, COO

Angel Rodriguez rose through the ranks of the organization. He has a reputation for getting things done without drama. That was why Shanelle made him COO. The two executives make an excellent team. Angel leaves the strategy to Shanelle and focuses on turning her visions into reality. He has more patience for internal politics among the leadership team than Shanelle, but only because he realizes he needs to be more a coach than a dictator. He believes he'll get more out of his team by giving them the space to be themselves, and so he's willing to cut everyone some slack. But if it looks like anyone's idiosyncrasies threaten to derail what Shanelle wants to get done, he's ready to be forceful.

Jabar Pyncher, The Penny Pincher

If you recall, Jabar Pyncher, the penny-pinching CFO, was the one the COO turned to for back up about the budget and who later raised the issue of long commutes. Jabar has never seen a cost he didn't think couldn't be trimmed. He thinks, *What's the return on investment?* Jabar never understands why anyone ever needs a team; he'll wonder why every project or initiative couldn't be done by one person. *And come to think of it, couldn't we just hold a town hall and issue an organization-wide memo rather than creating a new team?* If he's ever questioned, he'll say he's "just looking out for the good of the business." Jabar probably won't have any psychological or emotional reaction to any diversity mosaic effort. Instead, he'll view it as a transaction. Is it costing the organization more to do something different? If it is, he'll be against it. On the other hand, if Jabar can be shown that diversity mosaic efforts save the organization money or, better yet, will bring in an additional source of revenue, he'll become an advocate.

Stacey MacArthur, The General

Stacey MacArthur believes that everything an employee does must focus on the organization's core mission, whatever that is. Stacey's focus has often helped keep the organization from diluting its efforts. There are times when the organization could have been caught up in fads and fashions, but Stacey kept it on track. But Stacey sometimes doesn't understand how anything new will further the organization's mission. *How will it help us sell the world's best garlic press?* According to Stacey, the organization has limited time, energy, and resources, and anything not directly linked to the mission is a waste. Stacey will be resistant to new initiatives until she is shown that it contributes to the core mission. If she can be shown that the company needs a new perspective to ensure the success of the core mission, she'll go along with the effort.

Eric Luddy, The Enemy of Change

Eric Luddy is a veteran of the organization. He's the one who was so concerned about the company's traditional Christmas ham. Eric will respond coolly to any new initiative, noting how the organization has always done it another way. Eric will say, "We've never had a problem," and warn that the organization shouldn't "fix what's not broken." Every organization needs an institutional memory. Eric helps others address problems the organization has been faced with in the past by providing insight into prior solutions. That said, Eric may think that any changes are going to create problems, and he's apt to, consciously or not, throw up obstacles to prevent efforts from succeeding. Getting Eric to go along with diversity mosaic efforts will be a challenge. Nothing has ever gotten Eric to embrace change in the past, so we may not want to waste too much time and energy on the effort, at least initially. You can gently tap into his role as "organization historian" and point out that he has been able to weather all sorts of changes over the years.

Bea Crawford, The Narcissist

Bea Crawford always responds enthusiastically to every suggestion . . . at least outwardly. In private, however, her major concern is how any action or initiative will help or hurt her career. After you've left the scene, Bea will be thinking, *Are they saying that I might be at risk,* or, *Does this mean I won't be able to do what I want?* She will often be focused on her standing in the hierarchy, whether it's a staff of fifty or five. You'll need to show Bea how whatever change is being launched will somehow benefit her. For example, you can take advantage of her enthusiasm, even if feigned, and say the most diverse team in the organization will improve its image in the executives' eyes. At worst, you'll need to convince Bea that the acceptance of differences won't hurt her. That could neutralize any opposition. It's worth the effort to get Bea on board—narcissistic leaders are often the most inspiring people in an organization. If Bea believes in the mission, she'll get everyone in the organization behind it.

Aaron Brady, The Buck Passer

Earlier in this chapter, Aaron Brady ended the conversation about the holiday party by noting that the issue shouldn't be the leadership team's responsibility. Aaron will never speak out against any program, and that includes any efforts to expand the diversity of the workforce. He'll sit quietly during a high-level meeting and if pressed later, explain, without offering an opinion, that this isn't his job.

"That's an HR issue," he'll say, adding, "It has nothing to do with me." Aaron might acknowledge that there's a problem but think, *It's someone else's fault*, even criticizing the CEO (if she's not within earshot). One way to manage Aaron's buck-passing is to press him in the presence of Shanelle Lapides, the CEO, so he's unable to pass the buck without it hurting his standing. Another, less confrontational approach would be to make the project, or maybe an element of it, his responsibility by putting him in charge of it. However, don't forget that there's more to Aaron than these potential problems. He is always trying to ensure his team has the resources they need to complete their core responsibilities. And while he balks at his team taking on work he believes should be assigned to others, he's the first to volunteer to take on any work he believes fits within the scope of his team's role.

Jessenia Cannon, The Projector

Jessenia Cannon is personally supportive of every effort, but she consistently raises objections that may potentially be voiced by others. "Who is going to tell the difficult client that his team leader will not be at their ribbon-cutting ceremony because it conflicts with his son's school play? Who is going to tell the events manager that the traditional 11 a.m. boozy brunch has to be moved to 1 p.m. to accommodate employees who want to attend mass at noon?" While Jessenia can be exhausting because no one can please everyone all of the time, she is an excellent source of advice for other members of the leadership team. Jessenia isn't a spy, but her advanced insight on others is a great source of intelligence. Ask for her help in dealing with whatever objection she is voicing. Ask what she thinks the reasons are for the other person's objections. Ask for suggestions on how you might be able to overcome those objections. She'll be glad to help. Yes, it's like dealing with a child and their imaginary friend. But it's likely to work.

Theresa Stewart, The Saint

Theresa Stewart will agree the company has a problem, but not in *her* department. Theresa thinks departments that have no problems, like hers, should be exempt from any new programs. She's vocal about the need for others to work on their issues but thinks it's a waste of time for her to be involved. *Why don't they focus on the teams that have problems and leave teams like mine that don't have problems alone?* The truth is Theresa is probably right that her team isn't a problem. She is a model department head or division leader. If everyone on the leadership team was like Theresa, there would be fewer problems. You can use Theresa's sainthood as a tool by asking if she can serve as an example to the rest of the leadership team. Ask how she has been able to get her team to make these changes so seamlessly and request that she serves as an adviser to the other teams.

Jamie Little, The Alarmist

Jamie Little is always predicting doom and gloom and wants to debate the possible negative developments of any effort. She pays lip service to the need for an initiative and will smile and nod when someone above her in the hierarchy is in the room, but the moment they leave, the first words out of Jamie's mouth will be "what if . . . ?" She'll be thinking, *What*

will we do if this happens? What will we do if this doesn't happen? What will we do if someone gets angry? While Jamie may sometimes be overly pessimistic, her radar for trouble is often correct. An alarmist like Jamie can be more valuable than a cheerleading Pollyanna. Employ Jamie's attention to potential pitfalls by enlisting her to develop the to-do list for the diversity mosaic effort. Rather than viewing her predictions as reasons not to do something different, turn them into the hurdles that will need to be overcome since the project must be accomplished.

Max Yorkshire, The One-Upman

Back in the earlier dialogue, Max Yorkshire was the person who complained about having to pick up the slack for employees who had children. Max is usually silent when an issue comes up out of concern for his image. But once he feels safe to speak his mind, he'll become particularly strident and probably verbal. He's eager to compare his own experiences to those of others, always thinking how difficult things were for him and how easy it will now be for everyone who follows him. *No one helped me with this. No one helped me when I had an issue. I had to overcome problems on my own.* But Max's sensitivity about unfairness isn't limited to himself. He's quick to leap to the defense of employees who he feels aren't being treated fairly. You could ask Max to serve as an informal spokesperson for individuals coming into the organization who are different. Have him explain what it's like to face a problem without support. Draw on his "experience" for help in the diversity mosaic project.

Waylon Jones, The Brown-Noser

Waylon Jones won't wait for the initial meeting to be over before he voices his excessive enthusiasm for whatever efforts the boss suggests: "Great idea. Brilliant. Thank you for including me and trusting me to be a part of this effort." While Waylon's sucking up may be annoying, try to set aside his motivations and instead focus on what he is saying. A good idea doesn't become bad because of motivation. Whatever his faults, you'll be able to count on Waylon's support for any effort that he knows has the backing of the boss. Consider giving him the role of a "scribe" who'll put information together into a form for presentation to the boss since he likely knows the best way to frame things to ensure maximum executive support.

Mai Olaf, The Pollyanna

Mai Olaf is always smiling and supportive but, as a result, rarely offers any constructive comments. Tell Mai the building is on fire and she'll say that the office is now nice and warm and suggest everyone gather around the flames and make s'mores. She'll never express disappointment because she'll assume the decision *must have been the correct one.* You won't be able to rely on Mai for honest input about diversity mosaic efforts, but you can use her as a tool—for example, by teaming her up with Jamie, the Alarmist, to balance both of their tendencies.

Davis Orr, The Defender

Davis Orr is an icon for most of the staff. He has been a fixture in the organization for decades and is a favorite of the higher ups. That's because he believes the organization is perfect. Rather than throwing his support behind a person, like Waylon the Brown-Noser, Davis is the ultimate institutionalist: *I don't think the organization has a problem. Just look at our record of success.* Davis can be turned into an advocate for differences by framing efforts not as a way to correct mistakes the organization has made, but as initiatives to maintain the great work the organization has done in the past and to ensure continued success. Portray the organization as a leader in this effort, either in the industry or region, and Davis will be sure to support it. Davis may always see the best in the organization, but it can be important to have someone like that around. It's human nature for people to complain about their employer, whether it's warranted or not. Put a handful of employees together informally and it's apt to turn into a gripe session about the organization and its leadership. Someone like Davis, who is respected and views the organization positively, can help temper the almost reflexive antagonism some people have for their employer.

Reese Geller, The Control Freak

Reese Geller is extraordinarily driven. But sometimes, that drive is to check a task off the list rather than solve it. As soon as she learns what issue is to be discussed, she'll independently develop her own project plan and put it into place. Reese will assert herself in every discussion and look to promote her approach as the universal solution. She may try to preempt conversations so she can move on to the next item on the list that needs to be checked off. Reese can be an effective advocate for diversity mosaic efforts if you insist that she gets input from more cautious members of the leadership team. You'll also need to make sure that she realizes this isn't a one-time effort; it will be an ongoing part of the organization's culture from now on. That said, Reese is an extraordinary resource for the organization. Her boundless energy and enthusiasm mean that no task, not matter how daunting, will fall through the cracks. Her energy may drive you crazy sometimes, but her presence on your team ensures problems will always be tackled.

Carlos Brownsky, The Victim

Carlos Brownsky feels that while the issue or problem everyone is focusing on is important, there are other problems impacting him that are more important. He'll talk about issues he faces that could keep him from dealing with the issue in question. Carlos will think that the primary focus should be on dealing with things impacting him. To get Carlos onboard, you'll need to privately show him how diversity is the answer to a problem he soon will be facing. You'll need to reinforce that this issue takes priority over the myriad of other problems he'll be worrying about. Although Carlos's sense of victimization can be frustrating, it's important to remember that he may not always be exaggerating. In some cases, he may be raising legitimate concerns. Don't let Carlos's tendencies keep you from investigating claims. Think of him as an early warning system for organizational problems.

Danika Casper, The Wallflower

Danika Casper will blend into the background whenever an issue comes up. She may have a point of view but won't express it for fear that her support or opposition would seem self-serving. She doesn't want to call attention to her successes or to her failures. She thinks any attention could lead to problems. Danika is likely not going to do anything to detract from your diversity mosaic efforts, but she is also unlikely to contribute much to the project's success. She can be useful, however, as a tempering force if teamed up with one of the more dominant and aggressive personality types. There are times when office politics moves toward melodrama. Having someone like Danika around can help provide some calm when things threaten to go off the rails. Privately, you can use Danika as an example for how others can successfully deal with a situation. Make sure that she isn't overlooked and that her efforts are rewarded, and others might realize that you don't have to be the loudest person in the room to get attention.

Asa Lattery, The Procrastinator

Asa loves drama. She is motivated by crisis. Asa will ignore an issue or initiative until the last minute, but then will treat it as the most important thing facing the company. She is unable to focus on any task until it becomes an emergency. Asa will disappear into the background during early discussions and then dramatically emerge at the last moment to seize everyone's attention. Admittedly, Asa's procrastination can be maddening at times. But there are actually some benefits to the go-slow approach. It can actually improve efficiency by forcing more focused efforts. And time not spent getting a jump on some project can be devoted to other work that is important but that might otherwise be ignored. Asa isn't likely to have any philosophical or emotional issues with diversity mosaic efforts. She'll see it as one more chore to be postponed. Rather than trying to bring her along intellectually, work on her poor habits by teaming her up with someone like Reese, the Control Freak, who will force Asa into action.

Logan Brita, The Tactless

Logan has no filter. Logan will say things that others may be feeling but realize should be kept to themselves. Logan will make jokes that are inappropriate and, when confronted about it, will suggest that she is a truthteller whose honesty makes others uncomfortable. She makes group discussions difficult by cutting conversations short, not giving others enough time or room to express their feelings and discuss a solution. On the other hand, Logan's uncensored statements are most often true. Brutal honesty is still honesty. When you get Logan's support, you'll know it's complete and unreserved. One way to handle Logan is to bring her into your confidence as your special assistant in the project but insist that she must report directly to you with her ideas rather than to the group. Her lack of a filter will guarantee you'll hear every objection. And having her close under wraps could help keep her from alienating others.

Amy Bunker, The Lawsuit

Most organizations over a certain size are likely to have an Amy Bunker. You remember her from the hypothetical. She's the person who worried about the "war on Christmas" and who, probably purposefully, made a Muslim employee uncomfortable the year before by gleefully singling him out by wishing him a merry Christmas in front of the entire company. Amy is the person who tells sexist jokes in the break room, spreads whispered hallway rumors about peers' sexual orientations, and makes racist comments when she has too much to drink at the holiday party. She has been with the company for a number of years and is a fixture at the company, and many people are hoping she will find a new role outside of the company and move on. She may be tolerated because of her lengthy service and productivity. You don't need my superpower to know what Amy is thinking. It is going to be challenging to get someone like Amy to support, let alone advocate for, diversity mosaic efforts. Dealing with Amy is a conundrum for many organizations. The HR department and the lawyers will tell you to give her a stern warning and work to get rid of her at the next legitimate opportunity. Those who are very concerned with the bottom line may want you to just marginalize Amy, isolating her from the rest of the staff if possible, to retain her successes. The bad news is that dealing with Amy can be the biggest challenge you face in the organization. The good news is that there are fewer and fewer Amys in the workplace today.

* * *

Now that you know what your employees or peers are thinking about diversity, it's time for the next step in the process. You need to explain to the entire team holding divergent viewpoints that increasing diversity isn't about "out-groups" or others. It's about all of them too.

TAKEAWAYS

- Penny pinchers need to be shown that diversity efforts are worth the investment, have the potential to save the organization money, and/or will bring in additional sources of revenue.
- Generals need to be shown that new perspectives will ensure the success of the organization's core mission.
- Enemies of change need to be shown that they've successfully weathered changes in the past and that the organization is moving forward, with or without them.
- Narcissists need to be shown how diversity efforts will benefit them personally, or at least won't hurt them.
- Buck-passers can be neutralized by placing them in charge of an initiative.
- Projectors can be turned into sources of intelligence on others' objections.
- Saints can become used as examples or mentors to the rest of a leadership team.
- Alarmists can become the source of a comprehensive list of tasks and challenges that must be overcome.
- One-Upmen can be tasked with being a representative of new people or those without a voice in leadership.
- Brown-Nosers can be turned into scribes and spokespeople to frame efforts for higher ups.
- Pollyannas can be used to boost spirits and keep the team unified and moving forward.
- Defenders can help keep internal complaints and frustrations under control.
- Control Freaks can be harnessed to push through difficult periods and ensure that projects aren't left to languish.
- Victims can serve as an early warning system since their sensitivity may at times be accurate.
- Wallflowers can be used to calm troubled waters and keep more aggressive personalities in check.
- Procrastinators can improve efficiency by forcing teams to be more deliberate.

- Tactless individuals can be a resource ensuring that every objection or concern is being aired rather than ignored due to a fear of hurting feelings.
- Those who put employers at legal risk need to understand they need to adapt because their behavior will not be tolerated.

CHAPTER 3

DIFFERENCES AS
PROTECTIVE MEASURES

A workplace population that includes as many different characteristics from the diversity mosaic as possible, coupled with an organizational culture and structure that allows for free expression and widespread participation in decision-making, ensures diversity can serve as a protective measure—a life preserver for the organization. All the varied perspectives can keep your organization from making mistakes—both minor and major, internal and external. In this chapter we'll look at some mistakes organizations make that could be avoided if they had a more diverse workforce mosaic and a culture that encouraged input. But before we get into those stories, we need to acknowledge and address some critical issues.

* * *

As you read through the hypotheticals throughout this book, your initial reaction might be that they're ridiculous. *How could these people not know better?* Some might feel that an organization shouldn't need to have individuals with a specific characteristic involved in the decision-making to understand that a situation may offend or discriminate against someone with that characteristic. For example, an organization shouldn't need to have a disabled person involved in the selection of a new office location to realize the organization shouldn't rent space in a third-floor walkup with no elevator. That's true—the organization shouldn't need to—but initially, it might.

Everyone who is reading this book is mindful enough to recognize such decisions as mistakes stemming from an unintentional oversight at best, or a narrow perspective brought on by privilege, narcissism, or bias at worst. *But all these mistakes are happening.* Let me first cite some stories of well-known organizations that did incredibly insensitive things that you might find hard to believe actually happened.

* * *

In the summer of 2014, the American Red Cross, concerned with the safety of children in swimming pools, released a poster titled "Be Cool, Follow the Rules."[3]

Margaret Sawyer and her children were driving across the country in the summer of 2016. They regularly stopped at public pools along the way. Sawyer first saw the poster at a pool in Colorado. She initially assumed it was a remnant from a less-enlightened time. Then she saw the same poster at another pool, looked closely, and realized it was created just two years before. Sawyer took a picture of the poster and called out the Red Cross on Facebook. She also sent the photo to her brother John, a consultant in Washington, D.C., who posted about it on Twitter, calling it "super racist." The poster became a media sensation. Apparently, no one at the Red Cross who reviewed the poster before its release noticed that four of the five "not cool" behaviors portrayed Black children. A week after the story hit the media, the Red Cross ordered the poster removed from all its locations and issued an apology. However, the incident led the media to reexamine past Red Cross controversies about its responses to Hurricanes Sandy and Isaac and the earthquake in Haiti. The reporting also put the poster in the context of historic efforts to keep swimming pools segregated, further linking the Red Cross to racism.

* * *

---

3. To see the original Red Cross safety poster, see Peter Holley, "'Super racist' pool safety poster prompts Red Cross apology," *Washington Post*, June 27, 2016 (retrieved from *https://www.washingtonpost.com/news/morning-mix/wp/2016/06/27/super-racist-pool-safety-poster-prompts-red-cross-apology/* on March 23, 2021).

In 2017, it took Saladin Ahmed, a writer for Marvel Comics, to point out to Kellogg's that in a bustling crowd of Corn Pops, personifying a crowd of people on a Corn Pops cereal box, the only darker skinned corn pop was a janitor.[4] In his tweet Ahmed suggested this was an example of "teaching kids racism." While some in the "Twitterverse" took issue with Ahmed's response, others pointed out that while people might not notice it at first, once it was pointed out it was hard not to see the issue.

* * *

In January 2018, Swedish clothing retailer H&M decided to use a young Black boy to model one of their latest sweatshirt designs.[5] You would think that a company operating more than 5,000 stores in 74 countries and employing more than 125,000 people would have been able to tap into enough diverse perspectives to realize it would likely be problematic to picture a young Black boy in a sweatshirt with the phrase "Coolest monkey in the jungle" emblazoned across the front. The reaction was immediate and global: LeBron James was among dozens of celebrities who expressed outrage, the company's first store in South Africa was vandalized by protesters, and online petitions called for a global boycott of the company. While initial reporting about the incident speculated that a lack of diversity must have been responsible for the insensitive advertisement, that didn't seem to be the case. H&M did have an almost entirely white corporate structure but the company was quite diverse at all other levels, including the level that made decisions regarding the advertisement. What H&M apparently lacked was a culture that took advantage of its demographic diversity by being inclusive and empowering open expression of opinions. Internal and external analysis of the incident found that H&M's culture valued consensus decision-making and discouraged people from challenging group decisions.

* * *

---

4. To see the Corn Pops cereal box referenced here, see Samantha Schmidt, "Kellogg's apologizes for lone brown character—a janitor—on Corn Pops box," *Los Angeles Times*, October 26, 2017 (retrieved from *https://www.latimes.com/business/la-fi-kelloggs-brown-corn-pop-20171026-story.html* on March 22, 2021).

5. A photo of the sweater can be found at *https://www.nytimes.com/2018/01/08/business/hm-monkey.html* (retrieved on March 22, 2021). Liam Stack, "H&M Apologizes for 'Monkey' Image Featuring Black Child," *New York Times*, January 8, 2018.

And these mistakes know no borders. The high-end German appliance manufacturer Miele thought it was a good idea to celebrate International Women's Day with a Facebook post showing women reveling in their independence by gathering around a washing machine and dryer.[6]

* * *

Having someone with a rudimentary knowledge of Irish history as part of their organization might have helped Nike avoid its unfortunate St. Patrick's Day blunder. In 2012, the company decided to release a special Guinness-themed sneaker for St Patrick's Day that they named "Black and Tan."[7] The Black and Tans were a paramilitary unit notorious for committing atrocities in the Irish Civil War, including the Bloody Sunday Massacre of 1920. One commentator suggested it was like releasing a new sneaker called the al-Qaida on September 11. An awareness of this piece of history would also have been useful to Ben & Jerry's, which made the same mistake in 2006, calling a new flavor "Black & Tan."[8] Their response was that they weren't aware of the name's connotations.

* * *

There's also a long history of organizations that make terrible mistakes due to a lack of knowledge about other languages. Let's just look at beverage companies. When Coca-Cola first entered the Chinese market, it named its drink using characters that, when read aloud, sounded like *"Coca-Cola."* Too bad the characters translated as "Bite the Wax Tadpole."

---

6. To see the original Facebook post, go to *https://www.perzonalization.com/blog/social-media-fails/* (retrieved on March 22, 2021). Soner Alemdar, "Social Media Fails," Personalization, December 25, 2020.

7. For more information on this blunder, see Aisha Gani, "Nike puts foot in it with 'Black and Tan' trainers," *The Guardian*, March 18, 2012 (retrieved from *https://www.washingtonpost.com/blogs/arts-post/post/black-and-tan-shoes-force-nike-apology/2012/03/15/gIQAlYXGES_blog.html* on March 22, 2021).

8. For more information on this blunder, see Owen Bowcott, "Ben & Jerry's new flavour leaves bad taste," *The Guardian*, April 19, 2006 (retrieved from *https://www.theguardian.com/world/2006/apr/19/ireland* on March 22, 2021).

Pepsi fared no better in its initial Chinese campaigns. The characters used for its slogan, "Pepsi brings you back to life," actually translated into "Pepsi brings your ancestors back from the grave." The Coors Brewing Company slogan "Turn It Loose" was translated into Spanish as "Suffer from Diarrhea." And when Schweppes Tonic Water entered the Italian market, it translated its name into "Schweppes Toilet Water."[9]

* * *

Domino's thought it could bring some levity to a meme about a serious issue with a "Calling All Karens" campaign, offering a free pizza to people named Karen who wrote in and explained why they weren't a *bad* Karen—since the name is being used as a label for white women asserting their privilege.[10] More than one person pointed out the irony and insensitivity of offering free meals to people of privilege during a pandemic and recession that disproportionately impacted the poor and people of color.

* * *

Playing to the privileged during a pandemic didn't work well for Singapore Airlines either. The airline announced it would offer "flights to nowhere" for its typically affluent customers who weren't able to travel due to the pandemic.[11] The flights would take off and land at the same airport. People pointed out that it takes a certain kind of privilege and a total lack of concern for the environment to take a flight to nowhere for no reason other than to alleviate boredom. The airline quickly dropped that idea but then floated the concept of people being able to order airline meals and watch movies in grounded aircraft, placing the airline in direct competition with small restaurants struggling to survive.

* * *

---

9. For more information on these blunders, see "Cultural blunders: Brands gone wrong," *Campaign Asia-Pacific*, October 7, 2013 (retrieved from *https://www.campaignasia. com/article/cultural-blunders-brands-gone-wrong/426043* on March 23, 2021).

10. For more information on this blunder, see "Top Marketing Campaign Fails and Scandals of 2020," *B&T Magazine* (retrieved from *https://www.bandt.com.au/top-marketing-campaign-fails-and-scandals-of-2020/* on March 23, 2021).

11. For more information on this blunder, see Monica Buchanan Pitrelli, "Singapore Airlines drops 'flight to nowhere' idea but will let people eat in an A380," CNBC, October 26, 2020 (retrieved from *https://www.cnbc.com/2020/10/02/singapore-air-lines-drops-flight-to-nowhere-but-will-sell-onboard-meals.html* on March 23, 2021).

Bud Light, one of America's best-selling beers, would have benefitted from a more acute awareness of the #NoMeansNo movement before it came up with a label tag line they used as part of its "Up for Whatever" campaign.[12] The label said, "The perfect beer for removing 'no' from your vocabulary for the night." In effect, the label reinforced everything the movement was fighting against, including the connection between rape and alcohol.

* * *

While your first instinct may be that these mistakes happened in the past and we are living in a different world, these mistakes are still taking place. As I was writing this book, Warner Brothers released a streaming version of the Roald Dahl book *The Witches*, starring Anne Hathaway as the Grand High Witch. In Dahl's book and in the film, witches are portrayed as having "thin curvy claws, like a cat." Individuals with limb differences reacted with anger and sadness at the portrayal of people with limb differences as being evil, particularly in a family film.[13]

* * *

My purpose in highlighting some of these blunders is not to shame any particular company, but rather to show just how deep the problem runs. The fact that these missteps implicate such a wide range of characteristics supports the idea that all of us should share the goal of having an organization in which every employee, whether they have a particular trait or characteristic or not, is aware of all these potential issues. I'm confident we will get there as a society, but until we do, we need to accept that mistakes like these are being made by people who should be more cognizant of the needs of others.

---

12. For more information on this blunder, see Christopher Ingraham, "'No means 'up for whatever,' according to the latest Bud Light slogan," *Washington Post*, April 28, 2015 (retrieved from *https://www.washingtonpost.com/news/wonk/wp/2015/04/28/no-means-up-for-whatever-according-to-the-latest-bud-light-slogan* on March 23, 2021).
13. For more information on this blunder, see Rebecca Rubin, "Warner Bros. Apologizes After 'The Witches' Sparks Backlash from People with Disabilities," *Variety*, November 4, 2020 (retrieved from *https://variety.com/2020/film/news/the-witches-backlash-warner-bros-apologizes-1234823081/* on March 23, 2021).

In researching these and other real-world situations on which my hypothetical stories are based, I learned a lot about the wide range of circumstances that may have enabled these significant misjudgments. In some cases, there were people who didn't share the characteristic in question and sensed the organization was making a mistake, but didn't speak up. Why? Because they felt uncomfortable raising it since they didn't share that trait. These people thought they might not have an accurate sense of the issue, or that their opinion wouldn't carry the same weight as if they shared the perspective. They didn't want to take a risk and go against the crowd without having their feelings justified by personal experience.

Yes, our goal is to have an organization in which everyone feels comfortable raising concerns outside their own mosaic without fear of being perceived as a roadblock and putting their career at risk. But until then, we need to accept that even those who are aware enough to sense a problem outside their own experience may not raise the alarm.

While this situation may suggest that those who possess a characteristic are in the best position to educate others about potentially inflammatory decisions, this places an unfair burden on them. It's one thing to ask someone for objective input (*"Ali, when is Ramadan?"*). It's something else entirely to ask someone to subjectively serve as a representative of their group (*"Ali, how will Muslims feel if we serve hors d'oeuvres before sundown?"*). Why should they be placed in the position of having to represent an entire demographic, racial, or ethnic group? Why should their identity be reduced, even if just in this one situation, to a single characteristic? Isn't the whole point of the diversity mosaic that people should *not* be identified by one element of their identity?

Suppose your organization is hosting a gala and, to be financially responsible, is looking for ways to limit the number of complimentary tickets given out to the event. The Planning Committee is committed to providing tickets to employees and their spouses but is debating whether employees who are unmarried should also be given a second ticket free of charge. The Committee, in its wisdom, might look to the only single person in the room to ask how they felt about that cost-cutting measure.

For several reasons, the single person might not have a strong opinion on the matter. Perhaps they are not currently seeing anyone that they would want to bring to the event, or perhaps they are extremely social and prefer to attend events such as this solo. Regardless of how the single person feels, they also might not want to be designated as the office spokesperson for all single people. It is also possible that our single employee does have a strong opinion, finding the mere suggestion that only married people would receive an extra ticket to be offensive, but does not want to present their honest opinion because they do not want to be viewed as the person blocking cost-saving measures. Remember, also, that the key here is to create an inclusive workplace, and calling out a person based upon their differences might seem like step in the wrong direction.

In addition, asking people to serve as representatives of an underrepresented group places a workload burden on them. Ask anyone who is one of the few persons of color in an organization how much time they are now spending on things outside the normal scope of their job description because they're being asked to serve on various committees to ensure previously underrepresented groups are now represented. Today, if you are a member of an underrepresented group, odds are you are overburdened.

What is the solution? Employers should work to employ a diverse workforce who have the ability to spot potential issues, feel comfortable raising them, and can see that it is in everyone's interest they do so. The fact is yes, the ideal situation is we all "know" everything we need to know, and this would relieve both those who possess the characteristic being discussed and those who do not from any sense of discomfort. But we can likely all agree this is not the current state of most workplaces.

Eventually, your organization's culture will become more inclusive and won't need to rely on people with every trait in the employee mosaic being brought into every decision-making meeting. People will start to become allies and raise issues regarding characteristics they don't share.

They will realize that if they raise a concern for someone who isn't there, they will in turn be able to rely on their own concerns being raised by others even if they aren't in the meeting. A workplace with a growing number of allies will be able to impactfully lead your unified effort toward equity and inclusiveness. Have patience. This will eventually happen in your organization.

One way to perhaps speed up this change is to ask your team to engage in a thought experiment. Ask them to think about a time when one aspect of their identity made them uncomfortable. Perhaps they were the only woman in a business meeting. Maybe they were the only person without an advanced degree on a committee. They could have been the only single person at a party of married couples. Or they might have been the only one from a middle-class background in an affluent group supporting a local charity. Perhaps they were at a wedding in which they were the only person of a faith different than the bride and groom. Maybe they were the only vegetarian at a Thanksgiving dinner. How did they feel about being in this situation?

Then, ask them to think about how much more uncomfortable it would have been to have their difference dramatically pointed out and made an issue at the gathering. Ask them to consider how they might feel if that uneasiness never left them because those differences were consistently being pointed out, in all contexts, each and every day.

With this context in mind and the understanding that the examples that follow may seem hyperbolic but are unfortunately all too real, let's look at some mistakes that could have been avoided by having a more diverse workforce and inclusive organization. See the next page for a reminder of our cast of characters to help you keep track of the players.

Name		Motto
Shanelle Lapides CEO		"Make it work!"
Angel Rodriguez COO		"How do I make it work?"
Jabar Pyncher *The Penny Pincher*		"What's the ROI?"
Stacey MacArthur *The General*		"How is this relevant?"
Eric Luddy *The Enemy of Change*		"Don't fix what's not broken."
Bea Crawford *The Narcissist*		"How will this impact me?"
Aaron Brady *The Buck Passer*		"This has nothing to do with me or my team."
Jessenia Cannon *The Projector*		"I'm supportive, but how will others react?"
Theresa Stewart *The Saint*		"My team is perfect."
Jamie Little *The Alarmist*		"What if…?"
Max Yorkshire *The One-Upman*		"No one did that for me."
Waylon Jones *The Brown-Noser*		"Great idea, boss!"
Mai Olaf *The Pollyanna*		"Let's look on the bright side."
Davis Orr *The Defender*		"I don't think there's a problem."
Reese Geller *The Control Freak*		"I've already taken care of it."
Carlos Brownsky *The Victim*		"But what about my problem?"
Danika Casper *The Wallflower*		"…"
Asa Lattery *The Procrastinator*		"I'll get to it."
Logan Brita *The Tactless*		"I tell it like it is."
Amy Bunker *The Lawsuit*		"Don't be so PC."

Guess who's making mistakes.

This has nothing to do with me or my team.

Aaron Brady
The Buck Passer

Everyone had seen the new-hire orientation training videos and thought they were a huge improvement. Aaron Brady, the Buck Passer on the leadership team, had worked for months with an outside agency to create a series of online videos. The team, particularly Jabar Pyncher the Penny Pincher, was initially worried that Aaron couldn't keep within the budget and still get the results he was promising. But the agency had found a collection of affordable stock photos that could be used to provide visuals for the slides, which meant the company did not have to spend the funds earmarked for the hiring of a photographer. The videos were all completed and uploaded in time for the new group of employees to be brought onboard and trained.

In addition to creating the videos, the team was also committed to increasing the diversity of the staff. Several clients had pointed out to Angel Rodriguez, COO, that other than one Asian field salesperson, the organization's entire sales team was white. The clients had explained that as part of their own diversity efforts they were trying to ensure they did business with diverse organizations. And while the organization had a woman CEO and a few women executives, it had very few racial minority employees. In response, the recruiting team had been advised to look for diverse candidates.

It only took two days for the new recruits to start commenting on the training videos. Yes, there were stock photos of African American, East Asian, Hispanic, and South Asian males and females. But it turned out that almost every example of negative or problematic behavior or mistake was illustrated with a stock photo of someone who appeared to be a racial minority. And the manager correcting them was almost always a white male or female.

Aaron blamed the agency, noting that it had written scripts that focused only on mistakes and problems and that the agency had selected the stock photos. One recruit, upon hearing Aaron's justification, commented that perhaps the organization should have hired an agency that was itself diverse. The embarrassed CEO held a meeting with all the recruits, apologized profusely, and said the organization would return to the old written training materials, scrap the new training videos, and create entirely new ones with the help of a different agency for the next class of recruits. Angel asked all the recruits who had commented on the videos to join the project team to create the next set of videos. Jamie Little, the HR director who is the Alarmist on the leadership team, worried that it would now be doubly hard to recruit diverse people since word would spread about the training video debacle.

Since increased diversity was a stated goal of the new recruiting drive, the organization should have been more sensitive and self-aware. It could have compensated for its leadership team's lack of diversity in the short term by ensuring that it hired outside vendors and consultants that were diverse.

Excessive *Voluntary* Contributions

Theresa Stewart
The Saint

Theresa Stewart, the Saint on the leadership team, thought nothing of it when she announced to her department that she would be collecting contributions for a retirement present for Grace, her long-time executive assistant. Grace loved silk scarves—they were a regular element of her work outfits for more than a decade—so Theresa thought a new scarf would be wonderful goodbye gift. She found a beautiful Bulgari scarf for $500. Theresa, who earns a six-figure salary and who is married to a physician, didn't think twice about the cost. After all, it would only come to $25 from each member of the department. Theresa also didn't think to reach out to others in the department for their input or perceptions about the cost of the contribution.

The newest member of the staff, Jason, had just come on board as an assistant. He was earning less than $25,000 a year, paying off student loans for tuition at the local state college, and living in an apartment with his parents and two younger siblings, helping to pay the bills. That

$25 represented more than Jason paid for his lunches in a week. The previous assistant, Marci, was the daughter of another member of the leadership team. She had left to go to graduate school. When Theresa went from person to person to collect the $25, Jason was embarrassed to say he didn't have that much with him. He didn't feel comfortable explaining his situation and instead promised to bring the money in the next day. Theresa didn't notice that Jason skipped lunch for the next week.

When Jason left after only six months in the job, Theresa was surprised and upset. He had been doing a great job and Theresa had mentioned to him that he could have a bright future with the company. After he was gone, the director of HR came to Theresa to discuss Jason's exit interview. Jamie Little, the alarmist HR director, told Theresa that Jason felt belittled and demeaned by the rest of the department. Jason said that because he didn't come from an affluent family like his predecessor, no one respected him. Jason told Jamie he'd be posting a review on *Glassdoor .com* about his experience.

Theresa had just assumed that everyone in the department would find the $25 contribution as small as she did. She'd been used to a staff consisted entirely of people from comfortable, upper middle class and affluent families. Even though the prior assistant made no more than Jason was making and was also living at home with her parents, her economic circumstances were far different. Had Theresa been exposed to a more economically diverse group of employees and given more thought to soliciting funds for a gift for Grace, she could have avoided losing Jason and having him publicly comment about his poor employment experience with the company. Theresa could have asked people to anonymously contribute whatever they were comfortable with and then selected a gift based on the total. Or, if she was set on buying Grace the scarf, she could have contributed more on her own. The key would have been letting each member of the department contribute what they wished and enabling them to do so anonymously. While Jason's economic circumstances might have been obvious to anyone who knew much about him, there's also no way of knowing what economic hardships others might be experiencing in silence.

Good Intentions and Bad Perceptions

I don't think there's a problem.

Davis Orr
The Defender

For almost ten years, Davis Orr, known to be an unswerving defender of the organization, had headed up its charitable efforts. He looked forward to coming up with new drives that attracted community attention and highlighted how seriously the organization took its role as a responsible corporate citizen. The board loved the positive publicity his efforts brought, and the leadership team had taken to approving whatever ideas he came up with.

Davis was struck by a local news story about how many children were going without a hot lunch due to schools being closed due to the coronavirus pandemic. Drawing on his contacts in the community, Davis found a local franchisee of a major chain who was equally impacted by the hot lunch news story and was willing to partner with Davis and the organization to help address the problem. Davis ran the idea by the leadership team, which gave its usual rubber stamp to his ideas. The next week, Davis and a group of volunteers from the organization, all wearing T-shirts with the organization's logo, were out every lunch hour, delivering chicken sandwiches provided by the local franchisee. Mai Olaf, the organization's director of marketing, arranged for a local newspaper and a local television channel to cover the sandwich distribution. At the end of the first week, Davis reported the results to the leadership team, who were looking forward to the glowing media coverage.

The initial articles and television segment were very positive, but the subsequent public response was unexpected. Unbeknownst to Davis or the rest of the leadership team, the franchise's parent company had a reputation for being antagonistic toward the LGBTQ community. The newspaper and local news websites were filled with comments and letters to the editor calling out the organization as being homophobic. Mai, always a Pollyanna, tried to say that there was no such thing as bad publicity. Davis admitted he was shocked at the response since the national chain was well known for its charitable efforts. He suggested that this was just a minor problem and that it would be overwhelmed by positive responses to the organization's planned holiday drive. He was planning to have employees serve as bellringers for the fundraising efforts of a century-old international charity.

Not having the perspective of a member of the LGBTQ community among those reviewing Davis's efforts led the organization to see its charitable effort backfire and result in negative publicity. Continuing to lack that point of view threatens to become an even larger problem, since the century-old international charity is also viewed negatively by the LGBTQ community.

Wardrobe Malfunction

How do I make it work?

Angel Rodriguez
COO

Angel Rodriguez, the COO, was thrilled when Jabar Pyncher, the CFO who was known to be frugal, volunteered to take on the project of getting new uniforms for the organization's softball team. Jabar was almost always opposed to spending money on anything extraneous to operations. Angel thought that Jabar's willingness to support the organization's most popular extracurricular activity might be a sign his tightfistedness was easing.

Three weeks later, Jabar explained that by working with the representative of a sporting goods supplier, they were able to develop a design that combined the organization's present and history in a way that resulted in an attractive shirt. The shirt was primarily thin blue and white stripes that looked a little like a French sailor's shirt, echoing the organization having been founded by a former French naval officer. On the upper right chest of the shirts there would be a yellow six-pointed star patch that was one of the elements in the organization's current logo. He passed a sketch of the projected design around the leadership team and everyone agreed that it looked fine. Jabar couldn't help adding that he was able to get both the striped shirts and the star patches for a very good price since the sporting goods company had an excess of both in stock.

When Shanelle Lapides, the CEO, and Jabar presented the new uniforms to the team, everyone seemed happy. A couple of players mentioned that they thought there was something familiar about the design, but they couldn't place it. It was only the next day, when the team took the field for their first game of the season, that the familiarity became clear. Two players on the opposing team were appalled at the new uniforms. They were so offended that they cancelled the game. Angel, who coached the team, didn't understand at first, but then one of the players on the other team showed him a picture on their phone. The organization's uniforms bore a remarkable likeness to the clothing worn by Jewish inmates in Nazi concentration camps.

When the issue was raised at the leadership meeting two days later, Jabar sheepishly reported that the uniforms weren't returnable—"that was one of the reasons we got such a good price."

"I think we all now know another reason," snapped Logan Brita, never one to hold her tongue.

"You signed off on the design just like the rest of us," noted Davis Orr, rising to Jabar's and the company's defense.

If there had been someone Jewish or someone knowledgeable about Jewish history involved in the decision-making, the organization never would have outfitted its softball players in uniforms that made them resemble concentration camp prisoners.

Time and Technology Trouble

Jamie Little
The Alarmist

Jamie Little, the HR director with a reputation for being something of an alarmist, was surprisingly calm when she reported on plans for the organization's required sexual harassment training. Knowing that there were several employees who did not have computers at home, Jamie had arranged for a state-accredited trainer to come to the office and provide live classes. She was beaming at the weekly meeting as the rest of the leadership team praised her prudence in accommodating those without computers at home.

The next week, announcements were made about when the mandatory training would take place. It noted that there were classes set up every hour from 10 a.m. to 3 p.m. on two days later that month. The next morning, there was an email marked urgent waiting for Jamie. It was from Jessenia Cannon, who managed the unionized custodial staff employed by the organization. She pointed out that the custodial staff was scheduled 24 hours a day, from 8 a.m. to 4 p.m., from 4 p.m. to midnight, and from midnight to 8 a.m. That meant that two-thirds of the team would not be able to attend live training sessions.

Jamie picked up the telephone and pleaded, "Couldn't they stay late, or come in early, to make the sessions?" Jessenia pointed out that the custodians couldn't do that without violating contractually agreed schedules. Jamie asked if the custodians could do online training if she arranged it. Jessenia pointed out that many of them, just like other groups of employees, did not personally have access to the technology necessary. She also noted that the union rep for the custodians had called and complained that this wasn't the first time the organization had failed to consider the needs of its unionized employees. The rep was considering raising the issue with the union leadership and filing a formal complaint.

If the leadership team realized the need to get the perspective of its unionized staff, it could have come up with a solution and avoided animosity and potential labor problems. For example, printed training materials could have been prepared to provide the staff with another option. This way, everyone could have been given the choice to attend a live session, go through the training online, or use the printed training materials.

Trained to Leave

Reese Geller
The Control Freak

Reese Geller, the organization's Control Freak, was put in charge of choosing what type of external training classes to provide to the staff as part of the new program that Jamie Little, the HR director, was developing. Reese jumped into the project, researching different subjects, studying which were the best received, and which boosted employee engagement. Knowing the organization was desperate to increase retention, she put together a focus group of junior staffers to get their opinions. Reese discovered that the staffers gave the highest marks to two courses: one on crafting LinkedIn profiles and the other on writing up-to-date resumes. In her typical steamroller manner, Reese studied the options for courses that covered these topics, pressed Jamie to budget the funds needed to put them in place, and presented her plan as if it was a done deal at the next leadership meeting.

It was as if Reese had thrown a hand grenade into the conference room. Jessenia Cannon blurted out, "Who's going to tell the managers that we're helping their staffers leave? They're already worried about turnover."

Most of the other members of the leadership team agreed. Even Danika Casper, who typically said nothing at the meetings, raised concerns: "I thought we wanted to retain people, not help them leave."

Jamie, who was familiar with the same studies that Reese had read, tried to reassure the rest of the team, noting that the younger staffers didn't join the organization with the intent of spending the rest of the career with the organization. Young staffers appreciated support in developing their professional skills, and this kind of effort would reward the organization in the long term as it developed a reputation as a supportive, nurturing, and empowering employer.

Stacey MacArthur, who viewed everything through the focus of the organization's core mission, brought up the potential conflict among staff.

"The young staffers who don't plan on being here long might think these are great," she admitted. "But the veteran staffers, the ones who have been here for years and whom we rely on the most, want to stay here. They're going to see these courses as worthless at best or, at worst, as a hint to leave."

Had Reese put together a more diverse focus group consisting of long-tenured as well as newer employees, she would likely have come up with a different solution. For example, she could have suggested the organization offer one course designed to meet the needs of longer tenured employees, such as retirement planning, and another to meet the needs of the newer employees, such as crafting LinkedIn profiles.

What does casual mean?

Asa Lattery
The Procrastinator

Asa Lattery had been hearing whispers that people were talking about one of her new hires, Beth. Known as a procrastinator, Asa had chosen to let things go . . . because she could. Then, at a weekly leadership meeting, Shanelle Lapides, the CEO, said that she had heard there was concern about how a new hire, Beth, was dressing on the company's casual Fridays. Angel Rodriguez, the COO, explained that while he had not personally seen how Beth was dressing, he had heard from several people that Beth was taking "casual" to a new level. Asa immediately realized that she had to say or do something. She had the feeling that Eric Luddy, who hated anything new, was the one whispering in Angel's ear. However, it was Waylon Jones, the company Brown-Noser, who "seconded" Angel's concerns.

"I've heard the same things, Angel," he said. "You're right that we have to do something."

Looking to give herself more time to think, Asa asked for specifics. Waylon was happy to respond. "Last Friday she was wearing a tank top, cut-offs, and flip-flops. That's not appropriate."

Asa asked Waylon what he wore on casual Fridays.

"A tennis shirt and khakis," he answered, adding "typical business casual." Turning from Waylon, Asa told Angel that she would speak with Beth and get back to the group.

The next day was a Wednesday, and Asa found Beth wearing well-tailored blue jeans, a stylish blouse, and designer heels. Beth looked like most other professional women under the age of 30 in this post-coronavirus environment. Thinking there was no easier way to broach the subject, Asa explained to Beth that a few people had commented on the casualness of her Friday clothing. Beth seemed surprised and embarrassed. She said she didn't realize there was such a strict dress code. She took the phrase "casual Friday" at its meaning: she wore what she would have worn if she was going out with her friends on the weekend. Beth was apologetic. So was Asa, realizing that the policy needed to be clearer.

At the next leadership meeting, Asa reported on her conversation with Beth. Asa asked when the policy had been written. Jamie from HR said that it had been this way in the ten years she'd been with the company. Amy Bunker piped up that the policy was first written by the founders twenty years ago, and that at the time it meant jackets and no tie rather than the usual suit and tie for men and pants, rather than skirts, for women. It was soon obvious that the interpretation of business casual varied based on generation. The organization needed to come up with a clearer definition of what was not appropriate casual attire. Asa suggested that Beth be included in the group that would develop the definition.

Striking Out

Shanelle Lapides
CEO

Shanelle Lapides, the CEO, made a rare appearance at a leadership meeting in order to make a special announcement: The organization was looking into renting a box at the local stadium for the minor league baseball season. As a huge baseball fan, Shanelle thought that it would be great for employee morale and be good for marketing as well. Angel Rodriguez, Bea Crawford, Davis Orr, and Amy Bunker, who were also baseball fans, were vocal in their approval. Waylon Jones, who didn't follow sports at all, joined in with the approving voices when he saw Shanelle's enthusiasm. The rest of the group, including those like Logan Brita and Reese Geller who were never shy about offering their opinions, smiled wanly. Shanelle rode the apparent approval out the door, leaving the group to get on with the meeting.

Two hours later, the first cracks began to appear. Jamie Little, always the alarmist, came into Angel's office and said that she didn't think many employees would find the idea of going to minor league baseball games that appealing. Angel brushed off Jamie's objections until he heard the same thing from Reese, Jessenia Cannon, Stacey MacArthur, and Theresa Stewart. When Mai Olaf, Max Yorkshire, and Carlos Brownsky separately said the same thing later that day, Angel knew he had a big problem.

Not wanting to approach Shanelle without an alternative, Angel called Jamie and Mai to his office to brainstorm a solution. Jamie explained that not only would baseball tickets *not* bring the organization together, it could also hurt morale by signaling that the organization supported the interests of a few select people rather than everyone. Angel said he couldn't see how the organization could please everyone, and that maybe they should just give up on the idea. Mai said there was an alternative. She agreed that it was a good marketing idea to support the community, but the problem was picking one interest over others. She suggested buying a box at the local performing arts center. In any given year, the center hosted dramas, musicals, concerts, dance recitals, films, and even lectures. Not every employee might find something they were interested in, but it demonstrated the organization was trying to reach out to diverse interests.

Three is a crowd.

Angel Rodriguez
COO

Having weathered a difficult conversation with Shanelle Lapides about why her idea of buying a box of seats for the local baseball team wasn't a good idea, Angel Rodriguez thought the issue was behind him. The organization had announced its support for the local performing arts center and included a calendar of all the varied events. The idea received universal approval from the staff, and it garnered positive media attention as well. Ironically, the widespread approval led to another problem.

As part of the program, the organization said that each employee could put in requests for two tickets to an event each year. If there were extra tickets available to an event, people who had gone to earlier events before could request more. When the list of events was provided to the staff, employees immediately began requesting tickets. Those available for the plays, concerts, and lectures were allocated without issue. But when it came to the musicals and the local ballet company's holiday performance of The Nutcracker, problems came up.

Employees with children were upset to learn that they could only request two tickets. That meant it wasn't possible for both parents to attend with a child, and if they had more than one child, they would have to choose which to bring to the event. The larger the employee's family, the angrier they seemed to be by the limitation. Angel, who was single, and Jamie Little and Mai Olaf, whose children were grown, hadn't focused on the problem employees with children would face in attending events. When told of the issue, Shanelle, who had three younger children of her own, decided she'd approve the organization buying additional tickets for The Nutcracker so larger family groups could attend.

Boys will be boys.

Carlos Brownsky
The Victim

After the issues that came up with the organization's external training the year before, Carlos Brownsky was tasked to take the management of the process off Reese's hands. Afraid of being blamed for any potential problems, Carlos reached out to several local professional service companies—accountants, financial planners, insurance agencies, and law firms—and asked if they had any training sessions they could offer to the organization's employees. He figured that this way, the organization might not have to pay, and if there were any problems with the courses, he wouldn't be blamed. Remembering the issue Reese faced, Carlos asked two members of his team—Francisco Walsh, a long-tenured employee, and Adrian Venegas, a new hire—to serve as his focus group.

Carlos, Francisco, and Adrian reviewed the various packages from the firms and settled on a set of classes offered by the local office of a well-known financial services firm. The stockbroker who headed up the local office said that if Carlos's organization provided the conference room and refreshments, the financial services firm would conduct the classes at no charge. Thrilled, Carlos thought he had all his bases—and his back—covered.

When the class list was presented to the organization, there didn't seem to be any issues. People immediately began going through the offerings, looking for classes that appealed to them. Carlos was beaming. But there was a growing murmur as several employees began leaning to their neighbors in the room, exchanging comments. One of the recently hired employees raised her hand.

"I see that there's a course here called 'Investing for Women.' How are women's finances any different than men's finances?" she asked.

From the number of heads now bobbing in agreement, Carlos realized it was a rhetorical question. He tried to explain that these were the financial services firm's standard class offerings and that neither he, Francisco, or Adrian had anything to do with the selection.

"But the three of you did select this firm," Logan Brita noted. "I don't think we should work with a firm that displays a sexist attitude toward finances," she added.

Carlos apologized, said they would go back and review the other firms' offerings, and realizing his mistake, asked if Bridget, the woman who had initially raised the issue, would be able to join the team in reviewing the classes. She agreed.

If Carlos had assembled a team with a broader diversity mosaic, including women as well as men, or if he, Francisco, or Adrian had more experience hearing about both intentional and unintentional gender bias, the organization could have avoided the problem. At the very least, if Carlos, Francisco, or Adrian had enough knowledge to sense a potential issue, they could have reached out to the financial firm to ask them the rationale for offering the course and determine whether it made operational sense to proceed. At least this way, they would be armed with an appropriate response in the event the issue was raised.

Managers and directors first

Angel Rodriguez
COO

By 2 p.m. the local media was calling it the blizzard of the decade. Jamie Little burst into Angel Rodriguez's office and announced that the storm had taken an unexpected path during the morning and was bearing down on the metro area. Knowing Jamie could be a bit of an alarmist, Angel went out into the waiting room where there was a television that could be set to the local news. He found a bit of crowd already gathered there. When Mai Olaf, who never seemed to worry about anything, leaned over and suggested they have an impromptu leadership meeting to discuss what to do, Angel knew it was serious.

Jabar Pyncher, who had a long commute, announced that he would be leaving early. He added that Shanelle Lapides, the CEO, who also had a long commute, had already left. Reese Geller announced that she had already called a local hotel and asked them to put a temporary hold on a block of rooms for people who didn't want to travel and could pay for a room for the night. Amy Bunker made a joke about hotels, which everyone ignored. Stacey MacArthur said she'd also be leaving right after the meeting since she drove in, needed to get home to pick up her kids, and didn't want to make the trip if the roads were bad. A handful of people who lived nearby said they'd leave at the normal time and just walk home. Angel felt like everything was under control and went back to his office. He called his partner to let him know that he'd probably be spending the night at the local hotel.

An hour later, Jamie came back into Angel's office to announce that the city had just suspended all mass transit. Max Yorkshire came in to say that he was leaving to drive home and asked if Angel needed a lift anywhere. Before Angel could answer, Theresa Stewart came in and said that while her department had everything figured out, the administrative staff were very upset. Most rode buses from home to work and back. None of them could afford a room at the hotel Reese had contacted, and two were single parents who had no back-up childcare.

Angel, annoyed that no one had thought about the support staff's needs sooner, tried to reach Shanelle and Jabar on their cell phones. Neither was picking up. He called the car service the organization used, which told him they only had two vehicles available. Angel ordered the two vehicles for the single parents on the support staff, then used his phone to book Ubers, with his own credit card, for the rest of the support staff.

While members of the leadership team commuted in several different ways, none of them used local mass transit. As a result, no one focused on the needs of the staff who relied on buses or couldn't afford a hotel room. Angel's largesse kept the situation from turning into a disaster, but the support staff had been left feeling like they were stuck on the deck of the Titanic as everyone else boarded the lifeboats.

Unmasking Divisions

Asa Lattery
The Procrastinator

The requirement to wear face masks in the office to help prevent the spread of COVID-19 offered an unanticipated opportunity for political expression in a time of sharp divisions. Several employees started wearing masks that bore the slogan of one of the candidates running for president. Whether in direct response, or because they sensed an opportunity for their own personal expression, several other employees started wearing masks that bore the slogan of a new but rapidly growing social justice movement.

Seeing a chance for another dramatic role, Asa Lattery suggested she reconvene the team who had worked on the new business casual description in the employee handbook. She thought that the team had a good cross section of the company, representing many traits in the diversity mosaic, and so it would be able to come up with an effective solution. Unfortunately, the group split into two camps, modeling the dominant political split in the country. Each side thought the other's slogan offensive and their own acceptable. Unable to come up with a solution and worried the discussion would dissolve into an argument, Asa adjourned the meeting and brought the issue to the leadership group.

It was Mai Olaf, the marketing director, who came up with the solution: "Let's order face masks with the organization's logo and require those be worn in the office and when working for the organization."

Jabar Pyncher initially objected to the cost, but after hearing the cost estimates and being told it could be drawn from the marketing budget, he relented. Completely out of character, Danika Casper spoke up and suggested that until the logo masks were available, the organization buy a supply of plain white masks and provide them to all the employees.

Unfair Burdens and Benefits

Max Yorkshire
The One-Upman

When the coronavirus pandemic first struck, the organization did what it could to protect the health of its staff. After overcoming the issue of masks as political statements, an atmosphere of camaraderie and solidarity developed. But over time, the pleasant cooperation and teamwork began to erode. Until the coronavirus crisis, people weren't conscious of which employees had children, which were single parents, and which were childfree. Sure, people were vaguely aware of each other's familial statuses, but it wasn't at the forefront of most people's minds because it had little or no impact on work.

Max Yorkshire, known as the member of the leadership team who loves to one-up others, hadn't realized he was one of the only employees who didn't have children. When most everyone was working from home conducting business via Zoom, he initially had no problem filling in for others who faced childcare issues. His partner was a bit annoyed at times about how often Max had to fill in for parents who couldn't make meetings, but Max explained that his added workload wouldn't last forever. But once the Fall came around, and all the parents of school-age children faced having to supervise remote learning as well as handle their workload, Max's patience began wearing thin. Shanelle Lapides, the CEO, herself a parent of two high schoolers and a middle school student, had made clear the organization's support for working parents, particularly those with a working spouse, those who were single parents, or those who had no backup for childcare, by providing unlimited paid time off work for childcare necessitated by the coronavirus pandemic.

At that point, Max began speaking up about feeling taken advantage of. He noted that he wasn't being given unlimited time off work, and he pointed out that he was working longer hours in order to provide that time off to employees who had children. If you recall the hypothetical from back in Chapter 1, Max has taken to complaining about the situation during leadership meetings, especially when parents assert their needs.

Jamie Little, the HR director, let Angel Rodriguez, the COO, know that she had heard from the handful of other employees without children that they agreed with Max about how unfair the situation was. They were praising Max for bringing up the issue since they were afraid of saying something that would make them seem unsympathetic to their peers. They were noting that even though they didn't have children, they were facing added personal burdens too, while being required to fill in for those employees who have children. Had Shanelle brought a diverse group, including those without children, into the decision-making process early on, the organization could have come up with an approach that was more equitable, perhaps by offering some form of relief to every employee.

Refusing the Risk

Shanelle Lapides
CEO

While the virus was still a problem nationwide, the organization's state and metro area had done an excellent job mitigating the pandemic. CEO Shanelle Lapides and the board decided that the organization should enact a hybrid work plan. Employees would be asked to come into the office two days a week out of the six the organization was open. Angel Rodriguez and Jamie Little created a rotating schedule so the burden of coming back to the office was shared equally among the leadership team and support staff. Having been made aware of the unfair burden previously felt by the employees without children, Angel and Jamie made sure that everything was done to provide relief for everyone.

When the plan was presented to the staff over Zoom, the response was muted. No one was crazy about coming back to work, but most saw that the organization was doing what it could to be fair. Shanelle announced that the organization would follow the guidance of the local health department. If there was another spike in cases, the organization would return to entirely remote operations.

After the meeting ended, Shanelle received an email from Danika Casper. Surprised since Danika usually kept a very low profile, Shanelle was even more surprised when she read the contents. Danika explained that her elderly father, who had emphysema, lived with her. She said that she couldn't risk infecting him and was not willing to come back to the office and risk exposure until there was a vaccine available. As she was digesting the email from Danika, her phone rang. It was Amy Bunker. For years, Shanelle had been secretly wishing Amy would move on to a new role, saving the organization the problems of having to deal with her barely concealed racism, sexism, xenophobia, homophobia, and general abrasiveness. Amy was known by everyone in the industry and respected for her experience, but universally disliked for her curt manner and regressive attitudes. Amy announced that since she was diabetic, had heart disease, and had other health issues, she refused to come back to the office until she wouldn't be at risk. She added that she had spoken with an attorney who had assured her that her stance was not putting her job at risk.

Shanelle called Angel and Jamie to her office to discuss the situation. As they went back over the announcement, they realized their mistake. They had failed to realize that some individuals would not want to discuss their differences publicly. Shanelle said that in the future, any issue that potentially touched on personal issues would need to be addressed privately. Angel agreed. Jamie said that moving forward, they could send out private emails and establish a confidential means for people to respond.

Meanwhile, Jamie prepared a "clean-up" memo, apologizing to the staff and making it clear that in the future concerns would be addressed privately.

It's important to realize that there are many employees who may not wish to share information about differences publicly, while there are other employees who may actually be eager to publicly discuss differences. To make it more complex, employees may have opposite feelings about the same difference. The solution is to ensure that there is always a confidential means for employees to address their needs.

* * *

As you can tell from reading all these hypotheticals, having a diverse workplace mosaic and ensuring that as many mosaic elements as possible are represented in decision-making gives an organization the best chance to avoid disasters. While the focus of this book is diversity, it's important to understand that for diversity to serve as an effective defense, it's essential that the organization have a culture and structure that allows for free expression and widespread participation in decision-making.

Let's face it: It's unlikely that any organization is going to be able to have every element of its mosaic represented in its leadership team. Having an open and free structure and culture that encourages people to speak up for the needs of others can compensate for any gaps in the population of the organization's decision makers. When an organization encourages the development of mutual support and gives everyone a chance to express what they are thinking and feeling, it will be in the best position to prevent potential diversity disasters.

TAKEAWAYS

- Most times, organizations blunder due to a lack of perspective.
- There are times when people sense a mistake is being made but don't speak up because they aren't a member of the potentially aggrieved group.
- People who are part of a potentially aggrieved group should not be forced or pressured to serve as a representative, which reduces their identity to that single element and asks them to shoulder that burden.

- The solution is for people to become allies, raising issues of potential concern to others whose trait or group identity they do not share.
- Expansive allyship comes through the development of an equitable and inclusive culture.

CHAPTER 4

DIFFERENCES AS OPPORTUNITY GENERATORS

In the 1920s, Maxwell House Coffee, a Nashville-based company named after the hotel that was its first customer, wanted to break into the New York City market. Learning that there was no coffee that was certified as Kosher for Passover, Maxwell House Coffee decided to become the first.[14] The idea was to use Jewish customers to break into the New York market. Ten years later, to solidify its growing market share, Maxwell House's ad agency decided to publish a branded Haggadah, the prayer book that contains the ritual for the Passover seder meal. The Haggadahs were, and remain, free (on the honor system) for anyone who buys some Maxwell House coffee. In the years since the Maxwell House Haggadah was first published, it has become a cultural icon. More than 50 million copies are in print. It is used by families, schools, hospitals, nursing homes, prisons, and the U.S. military. It was smuggled as samizdat[15] into the Soviet Union and was used by President Obama at the White House Seder from 2009 to 2016. Buying Maxwell House coffee has become a part of the Passover ritual for millions of families.

The Maxwell House Haggadah is probably the single most effective use of a difference as an opportunity generator in American business history.

---

14. There are special dietary guidelines for the eight-day Passover holiday, which are stricter than the traditional Kosher dietary guidelines.
15. The Russian term used to reference the secret copying and distributing of materials banned by a government, especially in the communist countries of Eastern Europe.

It met an existing need and added value to customers lives. And it did so in a way that was authentic and restrained: as more than one person has joked, it was notable that Maxwell House did not modify their Hagaddah to include a prayer of thanks for the good coffee.

Your organization does not need to develop an approach or program as wide-ranging, long-lasting, or deeply impactful as Maxwell House's Haggadah to use a difference to generate opportunities—although let's face it, if you come across a comparable opportunity, you should grab it. Assuming such an opportunity does not surface, to tap into the power of differences, all your organization needs to do is keep an open mind and start thinking about differences as opportunities rather than obstacles. Here are some examples of how a variety of organizations used differences as opportunity generators.

LITTLE THINGS CAN MEAN A LOT.

When Brooke Walsh took over her family's business, she knew she had to be careful about changing too many things. For half a century, her family had run Klinge's, a unique retail store in a unique community. Located on a summer resort island in the Northeast, Klinge's was like an old-time general store. It was primarily a grocery store since the only supermarket was on the other end of the island. The only other shops in their little town were a chocolate shop, an antique store, and an art gallery. Brooke's grandparents and parents had always stocked whatever they thought their customers needed. Since it served a very affluent community, the store stocked things like artisanal pesto and single malt Scotch, as well as mousetraps, matches, and toilet paper. When Brooke started working in the store after college, she pushed for adding things like USB cables and hard cider, items she knew younger people needed or wanted. One thing Brooke wanted to change was to expand the store's reach to include residents from the neighboring town. The neighboring town was one of a handful of affluent African American resort villages in the Northeast. Over the years, residents of that village had tended to drive to the supermarket and shops at the other end of the island for their shopping rather than frequenting Klinge's.

Brooke had her daughter Masie work in the store on weekends, just as she had when she was younger. This summer, Masie had invited a college friend, Maya Bolton, to spend the summer on the island. Maya happily agreed to also work in the store on weekends. One day early in the summer, Maya was helping stock the shelves when she held up a box of bandages.

"It's always driven me crazy that they call these flesh-colored," she explained. Holding the box up to her brown skin, she joked to Masie, "not my flesh color."

It struck Brooke that she'd never focused on that.

"Couldn't you just buy clear bandages?" Masie asked.

"Who wants people to see the blood and everything else staining the gauze?" Maya responded.

"Would you actually buy bandages that matched your complexion?" she asked Maya.

"Oh, I do," she explained. "There's one drug store in my hometown that stocks all different colors of bandages."

That night Brooke went online and found the company that made the multiple-colored bandages. She saw that company sold a wholesale rack, containing all of its various shades, for a little over $100. That was more than twice what the store spent on bandages for a year. But while on the site she read testimonials from people who explained how much it meant to them, and their children, to be able to have bandages that matched their skin color. Brooke thought about it, but for only a minute. It wasn't much money. She didn't know if it would help attract new customers. After all, she wasn't going to advertise that she stocked the bandages. But after reading how people felt about the product, she thought it was just the right thing to do.

The display of bandages arrived three days later via UPS and they were on the shelf next to all the other healthcare products the next morning. That weekend an African American woman who wasn't a regular stopped in the store to buy a copy of the Sunday newspaper. She browsed the shop for a few minutes, paid for her newspaper, and left. Brooke didn't think anything of it. Later that week the same woman stopped by with her two children in tow. She bought some groceries, some firewood, and two boxes of the bandages. As she was paying, she thanked Brooke for stocking the bandages.

"It means a lot for my kids to see their skin color is included with everyone else's. I didn't see that when I was growing up."

As the summer progressed the woman and her family became regular customers. Brooke also saw a noticeable an uptick in the number of new customers from the neighboring village. One Sunday morning toward the end of the summer, the new loyal customer pulled Brooke aside and explained that after seeing the bandages, she'd decided to give Klinge's more of her business. She added that she'd told friends about her experience and suggested they do the same. Brooke thanked the new loyal customer and said she looked forward to seeing her next summer. Brooke reflected on how such a small investment could make a big difference and maybe result in an expansion of the shop's customer base moving forward.

What seemed like a little thing to Brooke was a big deal to people who never saw their needs or wants previously addressed. Acknowledging a difference in a way that is not obviously self-serving can make a big difference in people's attitudes toward your organization. Little things can have a halo effect for your organization. For example, Brooke's new customers will come to Klinge's for more than just bandages. Customers will want to support an organization that supports them. Don't feel like you need to search for dramatic changes to your organization to address differences. If you see a little thing that you can do, do it. Many people of color, for instance, say that integrating a store's cosmetic and hair care sections rather than segregating products designed for them in a separate section means a lot. You won't need to promote your efforts, either. Ironically, the less you do to promote these small steps, the more powerful they may become. The lack of promotion suggests that your organization is taking the step because it is the right thing to do, not because it's seen as a marketing effort. Rest assured that little things will organically reflect well on your organization.

WORDS MATTER

Prewitt & Scally Financial Services had begun as a storefront accounting firm. The two principals, Tina Prewitt and Linda Scally, had met in high school and always said that they had a shared vision and mission. They believed the minority community in which they grew up was severely underserved by professionals. The small businesses and individual residents either kept their own books and did their own taxes or relied on a major national chain that opened a temporary office at tax time and then vanished for the rest of the year. Tina and Linda believed their community deserved quality, personalized representation all year round. Ten years later, their vision, expertise, and hard work had resulted in the firm growing to six CPAs and more than a dozen support staff, working out of a former bank building they'd bought and renovated. Tina and Linda were now leaders in the community, sitting on community boards and committees, and working with bankers and politicians now eager to cultivate customers in the previously underserved neighborhood.

Always eager to support local youth, Tina and Linda regularly recruited recent college graduates whose families lived in the community. That's why Tina didn't think twice when she got a call from the local dry cleaner who said the son of one of his employees had graduated with a degree in accounting and was looking for a job. Tina was surprised when Sam Kim walked into her office. Intellectually she knew that there was a growing Korean American presence in the neighborhood, but to her that community seemed somewhat insular, especially since many were first generation immigrants who spoke mostly Korean, went to their own church, and shopped at their own stores. As she and Sam spoke, Tina saw that the young man shared the same vision and mission she and Linda had when they started the firm. Sam explained that many in the Korean community felt more comfortable working with people who spoke Korean and were travelling to another neighborhood, miles away, for their professional services. Sam thought there was a real opportunity for Prewitt & Scally to both bring the neighborhood together and tap into a growing potential revenue source.

Intrigued, Tina called Linda and asked that she join the conversation. Sam explained that he spoke Korean and could help recruit an assistant who also spoke the language. He suggested that with minimal investment, the firm could create a Korean-language version of its website and its marketing materials. It wasn't a matter of expanding its menu of services, Sam stressed. The Korean American community's only unique need was one of language. Tina and Linda thanked Sam and said they'd get back to him in the next couple of days. After he left the office, Linda burst out laughing. "Did he remind you of anyone?" she asked Tina, who started laughing too. They realized it was a no brainer: they could expand their market while breaking down ethnic barriers in the community. They hired Sam the next day.

Language is an all too frequently overlooked difference in the United States. Even though we are a nation of immigrants, there has always been a cultural and political pressure to speak English. Perhaps because of this pressure, companies' efforts to help non-English speakers have a powerful impact on the community. Focusing on language as an important skill when recruiting can provide unanticipated opportunities. For example, six months after hiring Sam, Sarah was interviewing for a new receptionist and was struck that one of the applicants was certified in American Sign Language. She realized this was yet another opportunity for the firm to use language to address an underserved niche market.

The costs of providing marketing and services in languages other than English is often minimal. Sometimes, it can even be done with technology or graphics. Providing pictures on menus can make non-English speakers more comfortable in restaurants. Alternatively, having menus or other sales materials printable in various languages can be very impactful. Audio versions, large-type versions, and braille versions can show respect for sight-impaired clients or customers.

CUTTING TURNOVER BY RECRUITING THE MARGINALIZED

Harper Salehi started the nonprofit Giving Galas after more than a decade as an independent event planner in a major metropolitan area. When she was on her own, Harper specialized in gala events for large corporations and major cultural institutions. A born obsessive, Harper had a reputation for cutting-edge events that went off like clockwork. She thought she'd achieved her business goal when she was tapped to plan and manage the inauguration of her state's governor. It was after that successful event that Harper began feeling qualms about the direction of her business. A local charity for children with learning disabilities, run by her good friend, approached Harper about planning their annual fundraising party. When Harper mentioned her usual fee, her friend's jaw dropped and she hastily apologized for taking up Harper's time. Harper, a fan of the organization, responded by saying she'd plan the event pro bono. Sitting and sharing a glass of wine with her friend after the successful party, Harper said that she hadn't felt so good about her work in years.

Harper launched Giving Galas as a nonprofit that would provide event planning services for other nonprofits. Instead of focusing on style and glamour, Giving Galas would focus on value. While continuing to run her own business, Harper hired her longtime assistant Audrey to run Giving Galas. The new organization took off. Requests were coming in from organizations all over the metro area. Audrey couldn't handle all the work, even with Harper helping when she could. They knew they needed to bring in additional staff but had a hard time finding people. Those who knew the business already were either focused on expanding their own businesses or lining up a job with a hotel, institution, or corporation.

Over dessert at the Thanksgiving table, Harper told her family about the problems she was having. Her father, a retired major in the U.S. Marine Corps, asked about the skills needed to be a successful event planner. When Harper explained the menu of skills, her father joked that it sounded like she needed a company sergeant. Harper's mother jokingly said no, what Harper needed was a mom who had three kids in school. They might have been joking, but Harper realized they both were right. The next day Harper and Audrey brainstormed about how to recruit veterans and stay-at-home moms who were looking to get back into the workforce. Working with a local recruiter, Giving Galas launched a hiring campaign. After a month, Harper had hired Ivy, a disabled former Air Force crew chief, and Sloane, a stay-at-home mom whose youngest was just entering high school.

Six months after hiring Ivy and Sloane, Harper and Audrey reviewed the results. Both had picked up the business right away and brought their own networks of contacts and innovations to the organization. Clients were thrilled to work with both. With fall on the way and new clients coming on board for the holiday season, Giving Galas returned to the recruiter they'd used to find another one or two planners. The recruiter told them they'd likely find their new employees extremely loyal: he said that hiring people who had a hard time finding work usually resulted in high employee engagement and low turnover.

FROM TODDLERS TO SENIORS

Ian Khan had gotten his start as a salesman for a high-end consumer electronics manufacturer. His "big idea," as he called it, came to him when his three-year-old daughter desperately wanted to play with his iPod. Like lots of toddlers, she loved listening to music but also wanted something of her own on which to play music, rather than relying on her father's machine. Over drinks at a trade show, he shared the story with a friend of his from a company that made specialty waterproof MP3 players for runners. His friend said his kids were the same way, and laughingly talked about how they couldn't manage to work the machines on their own. The light bulb went off over Ian's head: Simple Sounds—music players for children. He spent the rest of the trade show soliciting opinions and tracking down possible suppliers. It took two years and all his savings, but Simple Sounds came out with its first products, which were sold in specialty toy stores and online. After a successful first holiday season, he got orders from a national bookstore chain and a national children's clothing chain. He never looked back.

The Simple Sound players went through cosmetic changes each year and got some internal technical upgrades but remained much the same. Sitting down with his accountant one day, Ian admitted he was getting a little bored. The accountant scolded Ian for not appreciating that he'd come up with an "evergreen" niche product.

"Kids love them," he said, adding "Even my mother, who has Alzheimer's, can use the player."

Another light bulb went off over Ian's head. He scheduled meetings with two local gerontologists, and then enlisted his accountant and one of his salespeople to join him in visiting the memory care units of some nearby adult facilities. Ian brought his notes from those meetings to his supplier and had them put together a couple of prototypes. Soon he had his salespeople out test marketing Simple Sounds' new product line: music players for people suffering from Alzheimer's and dementia. The first holiday season for the new players was a huge success. Without any brick-and-mortar locations, Ian relied on online marketing and sales to push the new product line. He sold out his initial production run in two months and was soon in negotiations with a couple of drugstore chains that were thinking of stocking the players.

When asked about his second "big idea" by a business journalist, Ian was uncharacteristically humble. He explained that sometimes, all it takes is a fresh point of view to see that a product can serve an entirely different customer base. By focusing more generally on what needs a product addresses, he added, you can start to think outside the box and gain that added perspective. Ian realized that he could expand his customer base by focusing on caregiving as a variable element of his end user's diversity mosaic. They weren't just parents of young children; they were children of aging parents.

"I like the idea of addressing my customer's needs as they grow older: first they buy a Simple Sounds player for their child, and then a few years later they buy one for their parent."

TAKING ADVANTAGE OF THE HALO EFFECT

When Mary Ruppel took over as director of public relations for Rhett Corporation, she was struck by how little involvement the company had in the local community. Rhett began as a small local business and had grown to a nationally known corporation, part of the Fortune 1000. Its Chairman and CEO was the grandson of the founder, and he took pride in his family's involvement in the community. When pressed on the company becoming more active, he cited his grandfather's dictum that the best thing a company could do for its community was provide well-paying jobs for residents. Mary had tried to gently prod the Chairman and CEO by bringing charitable solicitations from non-controversial organizations to his attention, suggesting the company's support could make a big difference. Invariably, he said that his family's foundation would provide a donation, but the company would not. Mary tried to explain that the support of the company carried more influence than the support of just his family, but he remained reluctant.

Mary had been volunteering at the local SPCA since she'd moved and taken the job at Rhett. One day, when she was walking a dog who had just been dropped off at the shelter, she was surprised to find the Chairman and CEO's mother walking another dog on the same path. Mary introduced herself and the two began talking. The boss's mother was a zealous animal lover, and she and her daughter, the boss's sister, had been very generous supporters of the SPCA for years. She explained to Mary that her father, the boss's grandfather, was also a zealous animal lover, and had been one of the founders of the local SPCA. Armed with a new sense of the history of the Chairman and CEO's family, Mary decided to make another effort. But this time, she enlisted the help of her new co-volunteer.

A week later, Mary was called into the Chairman and CEO's office. He noted that his mother and sister had spoken with him about the needs of the local SPCA and they had pushed for the company to get behind the organization. He asked Mary to explain again why this type of corporate support would be better than his family's personal support. Mary explained that the involvement of the corporation carried weight outside of the community and could result in greater regional and national attention to the cause. She explained that the corporation's demonstrating a charitable impulse served as encouragement to other local businesses to get involved. Finally, she noted that corporate support boosted the image of the organization in a way family support did not. The company showing a charitable impulse would result in an improvement in its image. People who searched for investments in organizations that mirrored their own values would be attracted to the company. After a moment's contemplation, the Chairman and CEO agreed, and told Mary to make it happen.

Six months later, Mary was called back into the boss's office. The organization's generous support for the local SCPA, coupled with his family's historic support, had been reported in several media outlets, with Mary's encouragement. The company's newfound community activism was reported in an article citing its rise on a list as one of the best companies in America. The company was receiving new inquiries from investment funds that focused on social activism. Its stock price had risen. And the Chairman and CEO was getting new kudos when he had dinner at the local country club.

* * *

As these stories show, using differences to provide opportunities for your organization doesn't require you to draw on the demographics or characteristics of your staff. While the inspiration can come from within, it can also come from clients, customers, or even the world around you.

The secret is seeing differences as potential prospects rather than burdens to overcome. Just as openness paves the way for an organization to be able to avoid diversity disasters, so it provides opportunities to grow and develop.

TAKEAWAYS

- Organizations need to develop the understanding that different perspectives can help generate opportunities, not just avoid blunders.
- Realize that little things can mean a lot. Small efforts can have an impact that far outweighs their cost.
- Understand that words matter. Language is one of the most overlooked barriers in American society. Overcoming language issues is often inexpensive and simple.
- Recruit members of marginalized groups and turnover will drop. Individuals from historically disadvantaged groups show extreme loyalty to organizations that embrace them.
- A different perspective can put a product or service in an entirely new light, opening up new markets or customers.
- Efforts at increasing diversity can be beneficial in a number of ways, including boosting the organization's overall image.

CHAPTER 5

STRATEGIES FOR MANAGING YOUR ORGANIZATION'S MOSAIC

I hope the stories in the prior two chapters were illustrative of how embracing the diversity mosaic can both help your organization avoid disasters and take advantage of opportunities. To make it easier to put this approach into practice, I've studied these and other case studies and hypotheticals and developed a series of strategies based on them that you can follow in your own organization.

I'll be going over these strategies in this chapter. But there's a philosophy underlying all of them that's so essential, I think it's necessary to first discuss it independently so you have a foundation in place.

TREATING EVERYONE THE SAME CAN PERPETUATE ISSUES

Historically, the most widely accepted philosophy about how to help a group of people deal with an issue has been to treat everyone equally. After all, what could be fairer than doing the same thing for every person? That may make sense if equality is our goal. But it's not. Our goal is to address the issue, and in some ways, equal treatment actually perpetuates the issue. Let's dig deeper into what I mean by looking at a classic graphic example.[16]

---

16. For a comprehensive review of the origin of this image and its iterations, see "The problem with the equity vs. equality graphic you are using," Cultural Organizing (retrieved from *https://culturalorganizing.org/the-problem-with-that-equity-vs-equality-graphic/* on March 23, 2021).

Here are three people behind a brick wall that's between them and a beautiful scenic park. The issue is that the brick wall that encircles the park obstructs the idyllic view. In the first scenario, the three people are treated equally. None of them gets more help than the others. But because Person 1 is taller than the rest, they can see over the wall. The view of Person 2 is blocked, but maybe they could jump and get a quick peek. Person 3, however, is short and even if they jump, they'll never be able to see what's on the other side of the wall. This treatment may be equal treatment, but it does nothing to address the issue.

When someone, like our One-Upman, Max Yorkshire, complains that others are receiving help that he never received, it can help to explain that treating everyone the same isn't the organization's goal. Addressing the issue in a fair manner is what we should hope to achieve.

It is becoming widely understood and accepted today that rather than treating everyone equally, everyone should be treated equitably. Let's go back to our brick wall. Remember, the goal is to give everyone an unobstructed view of the lovely scene on the other side.

Because Person 1 can already see over the wall, they don't need any help. Person 2, who was forced to jump up for a quick peek, can be given the same view as Person 1 simply by being given a single block to stand on. With that help, Person 2 is at the same level as Person 1. Person 3 couldn't see over the wall if they were given a single block to stand on. Instead, they're given two blocks. Now, all three people have the same opportunity to see the scenery. The issue has been addressed through equitable treatment: each person has been given the help they need to see over the wall.

In our hypothetical, a few basic blocks represented an equitable solution. While this did address the short-term issue, it is generally not the best long-term solution. Why? Because it does not do anything to address the underlying circumstance that is causing the need for the unequal (but equitable) solution in the first place. Person 2 will always need one block, and Person 3 will always need two blocks to see over the wall.

Human beings are sensitive and imperfect creatures. Over time, Person 1 could begin feeling like they are being taken for granted because they're tall enough to see over the wall. Person 3 can begin to worry that they're being resented because they receive the most blocks to see over the wall. And Person 2 could begin to feel like they're caught in the middle because they need more help than Person 1 but less help than Person 3.

In the long term, the answer is to identify and resolve the underlying issue that is preventing everyone from receiving the same benefit. In this case, rather than helping the people overcome the brick wall that is blocking the view of the scenery, the best solution is to replace the brick wall with a mesh fence. The animals are still safe but now everyone can see the scenery without any obstructions and without any external equalizers.

Throughout this book I've tried to stress the importance of embracing a diversity mosaic with the understanding that differences involve more than just the legally protected categories. When most people hear or read about systemic treatment, they think of dealing with systemic racism, sexism, homophobia, ageism, xenophobia, or any other widespread established discrimination against a protected group. However, systemic issues have the potential to impact individuals across an even broader list of characteristics.

And just like we can all benefit from a commitment to increased diversity, we can all benefit from the elimination of systemic problems. It should be our collective goal to eliminate these systemic problems. Doing so will not be easy, but it is essential.

Systemic bias harms everyone, not only those being discriminated against. For example, voting restrictions harm students, the elderly, those without transportation, those living in rural areas, and those working for an hourly wage rather than a salary, not just those in protected groups typically seen as the targets of such constraints. Likewise, higher rates of arrest, conviction, and incarceration due to systemic bias hurt all those less able to pay for quality representation in the justice system, not just those in protected groups typically seen as the victims of such higher rates.

Studies have estimated that closing the racial wealth gap created by systemic racism would increase the U.S. GDP by four to six percent in the next decade; so in not addressing this, we rob all Americans of a higher standard of living. Systemic racism has also been cited as a contributing factor in wage stagnation, through the weakening of support for collective bargaining when the process is framed in ethnic and racial political terms.

The idea here is for us to do what we can to solve short-term issues by leveling the playing field in our organizations, while also looking for long-term, strategic approaches that work to resolve systemic issues.

With this in mind, let's move on to some specific strategies we can use right now. When tackling this chapter, understand that I know that your organization may not be ready for all of these paths forward. Don't let that keep you from reading the whole chapter, however. My strategies can help prompt you to develop your own variations or completely different approaches. All the management skills you've acquired over the years can be applied to creating and running your organization's diversity mosaic.

As I've said many times in this book, this isn't easy or comfortable and there are lots of potential landmines along the way, but at the same time, it's not rocket science. You already have the tools and skills you'll need, so don't shy away from tackling difficult situations. Ignoring a problem won't make it go away. All procrastination does is make a problem worse.

Assume goodwill on the part of everyone, but insist on accountability. Remember the goal: creating as diverse and inclusive an organization as possible.

Once again, here's a reminder of our cast of characters:

Name		Motto
Shanelle Lapides CEO		"Make it work!"
Angel Rodriguez COO		"How do I make it work?"
Jabar Pyncher *The Penny Pincher*		"What's the ROI?"
Stacey MacArthur *The General*		"How is this relevant?"
Eric Luddy *The Enemy of Change*		"Don't fix what's not broken."
Bea Crawford *The Narcissist*		"How will this impact me?"
Aaron Brady *The Buck Passer*		"This has nothing to do with me or my team."
Jessenia Cannon *The Projector*		"I'm supportive, but how will others react?"
Theresa Stewart *The Saint*		"My team is perfect."
Jamie Little *The Alarmist*		"What if…?"
Max Yorkshire *The One-Upman*		"No one did that for me."
Waylon Jones *The Brown-Noser*		"Great idea, boss!"
Mai Olaf *The Pollyanna*		"Let's look on the bright side."
Davis Orr *The Defender*		"I don't think there's a problem."
Reese Geller *The Control Freak*		"I've already taken care of it."
Carlos Brownsky *The Victim*		"But what about my problem?"
Danika Casper *The Wallflower*		"…"
Asa Lattery *The Procrastinator*		"I'll get to it."
Logan Brita *The Tactless*		"I tell it like it is."
Amy Bunker *The Lawsuit*		"Don't be so PC."

Look for a one-size-fits-all solution.

Don't fix what's not broken.

Eric Luddy
The Enemy of Change

Charged with setting up the organization's annual meeting for clients and customers, Eric Luddy didn't think the assignment would be difficult. After all, the meeting had followed the same blueprint for the past five years: a day-long series of seminars and round tables, facilitated by people from the organization, held at a local hotel. Eric assumed he'd simply take the previous year's plans and see what needed updating. Sales and Marketing were working on the content and invitations. All Eric and Operations needed to do was handle the logistics. Jamie Little suggested that Eric review the email survey of attendees taken the week after last year's event.

"I think there were some issues," Jamie warned.

Reading through the comments, Eric saw there were some complaints that the meeting had been held on a Thursday. Several attendees noted that they'd prefer that it was held on a Friday. Some others wished that recordings of the seminars and round tables were available. Eric knew that the organization had chosen a mid-week day and hadn't bought digital recording equipment due to financial concerns. Sales were down at the time and Jabar Pyncher, the CFO, had launched a cost-cutting effort that had the support of Shanelle Lapides, the CEO. This year, sales were up. During a brief discussion with Angel Rodriguez, the COO, and Jabar, Eric was able to get approval to book the hotel for a Friday and to purchase a quality digital audio recorder and a few microphones so MP3s could be created and either texted or emailed to the attendees right after each event.

It was the other set of complaints that was most concerning. There was always a luncheon for attendees. Each attendee group had their own table, and they were joined by a member of the organization who served as "the host." The meal was typical corporate dining room fare: attendees could choose a chicken salad or steak fajitas. Attendees complained about everything, from the lack of an opportunity to mingle to the dining choices. Many complained there was no vegan option and that there was no consideration of those who had dietary issues—some health-related and some culturally-related.

The organization's own issues with the holiday party were fresh in Eric's mind, so he knew how fraught this seemingly minor issue could become. He decided to put together his own brain trust consisting of salespeople who knew the clients well, the dining manager of the hotel, and Angel, who had handled the holiday party hubbub.

The group batted around menu ideas, but it was one of the salespeople who steered the group in the right direction: "We need to come up with an inexpensive solution that works for everyone, gives people a chance to mingle, and doesn't make us look tightfisted."

The hotel's banquet manager was going through the possible offerings and their prices when Eric, mindful of advice he received from Reese Geller to think outside the box, asked about all the offerings, not just the luncheon choices. Eric saw that the company could offer a self-serve, stand up breakfast buffet along with a self-serve, fruit and salad lunch buffet, for the same price as the sit-down luncheon. Rather than having an hour lunch break, they could schedule a 30-minute meet and greet breakfast and a 30-minute afternoon snack. The offerings could be vegan without being noticeably so. The banquet manager said the quality of the food would be higher since the options and preparation cost and time was limited. There would be ample chance for mingling and offering two dining opportunities made the organization seem generous.

The fear is often that looking for a one-size-fits-all solution to a problem means finding the lowest common denominator—something that annoys no one but also delights no one. However, thinking outside the box and focusing on doing something of high quality can make a one-size-fits-all solution seem like an innovation rather than a compromise. For example, many innovative organizations now offer paid time off as a one-size-fits-all bucket rather than assigned dates. Employees may receive 30 days of paid time off and are expected to work unless they use their time. The organization does not close for any holidays that it is not legally mandated to close. Employees can decide to take off a religious holiday, a day when their child is off school, their anniversary, the day of a major sporting event, or a week when they want to go skiing. While everyone's bucket is the same size, each is unique to their individual needs.

Delegate the resolution.

Davis Orr
The Defender

Having been burned by his choices when leading the prior year's charitable efforts for the organization, Davis Orr was not looking forward to this year's drive. He had already been warned that working with the religious charity as he'd planned would be problematic, but when he subtly sought to pass the task on to someone else, Shanelle Lapides, the CEO, told him that she knew last year was just an aberration and that Davis was the long-time face of the organization's charitable initiatives.

"The community expects you to be out front," she explained. With no comfortable way out of the task, Davis was thinking that he'd need to put together a focus group representing every possible type of person in the world to ensure he didn't pick a charity that offended someone.

Before developing a list of people and bringing them all together, Davis decided to speak with Aaron Brady. Aaron and Davis had been friends for years. Aaron was smart and effective, and he also had a well-earned reputation for being able to maneuver around political issues in the organization. Davis had always marveled at Aaron's ability to deal with potential problems without damaging himself. Davis asked Aaron how he could still get out of running the charity drive. Aaron explained that since Davis had already tried to get out of the assignment and failed, there was no way he could pass the buck to someone else in the organization.

"What you need to do is remain the manager of the task, but not be responsible for the ultimate selection," Aaron suggested.

The two brainstormed over lunch. Aaron suggested that maybe Davis could come up with a program that gave every employee a certain amount of money that they could direct to a charity of their own choice. Davis didn't think that was workable since there could still be controversies over charities selected by individual employees. Besides, by diluting the donation, it wouldn't have the impact or get the attention of the organization's usual single large contribution. But the concept intrigued Davis.

He started thinking about all the various charitable groups in the community and realized that there might be ways to delegate the selection of a charity.

At the next meeting of a community-based charitable organization to which he belonged, Davis asked if there was any type of charity wholesaler to whom he could delegate the responsibility. A couple of the other members pointed out that the local branch of the national nonprofit served in that kind of role. Donations were given to the local nonprofit, and that organization then allocated funds to deserving local charities and causes. Davis brought the idea to Shanelle and to Angel Rodriguez, the COO. Both enthusiastically approved the solution.

Delegating the resolution of a problem isn't necessarily an abdication or shirking of responsibility. Spreading the task out among a large group of people may not have been workable in Davis's situation, but it can be effective in some situations. The classic example is holding a potluck event. That guarantees no one at the event will go without having their own dietary needs met or feel left out. However, there are times when people will not want to assume the cost or burden of being part of the solution, or when it simply isn't appropriate or effective. Instead, as Davis discovered, it's possible to delegate a potentially problematic selection out to a person or organization that specializes in making these kinds of difficult decisions. A specialist provides the added advantage of offering expertise. Focusing on that expertise when explaining the delegation frames the decision as efficient, not defensive.

Expect to make mistakes.

Mai Olaf
The Pollyanna

Mai Olaf was thrilled when Shanelle Lapides, the CEO, asked her to be the point person for the organization's renovation of their new offices. Mai might be the director of marketing, but she was a frustrated interior designer, as everyone who ever visited her office knew. It was something of a running joke in the organization about how Mai's home was consistently under renovations as a never-ending project of love for Mai and her husband. The walls of Mai's office were covered with photos and drawings of the latest project and she never tired of telling people about the renovation underway.

Mai dove into the discussions with the builder who was renovating the new offices. She gave regular presentations to the leadership team, soliciting opinions and ideas. She also opened the discussions up to the entire staff and asked everyone to not hesitate to bring up any concerns or needs.

"We spent so much time working remotely due to COVID-19, and now that we're going to be back in the office, I want all of us to think of the new office as our home away from home."

Mai knew the organization had one employee who used a wheelchair and a new hire who identified as nonbinary. Mai stressed to the builder that the organization cared a great deal about diversity and accessibility and wanted the floor plan to address that. The builder said she understood and would incorporate those needs into the plan.

When the first draft of the floorplan was presented to the leadership team, everyone seemed enthusiastic. There were mostly small private offices, which was becoming the new norm in the post-COVID office world, but there were also lots of small conference rooms and snack rooms. The bathrooms were handicap-accessible and there was a single gender-neutral bathroom. Because she did not want to put any of the staff people in an uncomfortable situation, Mai decided to send the proposed plans out to employees via email and requested feedback through that channel as well.

Mai was surprised when the non-binary employee appeared outside her door the next day.

"I feel like I'm being singled out," Carlos explained. "You might as well have put my name on that single gender-neutral bathroom. It's embarrassing. It's not like there's a single handicapped bathroom for Jerome."

Mai was stunned. She'd thought she had deftly handled the issue. She quickly apologized and said she'd get back to them.

She set up a conference call with the builder, Angel Rodriguez, the COO, and Shanelle Lapides, CEO, the next day. Explaining the situation, Mai apologized for making a mistake and asked for suggestions. Shanelle eased Mai's conscience.

"This kind of situation is new to many of us," she noted. "Let's just talk it through and come up with a solution."

Angel mentioned how Eric Luddy had solved a diversity problem by looking for a one-size-fits-all solution. Mai mentioned Carlos's citing that every bathroom was handicapped accessible.

"What if every bathroom was non gender specific?" she asked.

The builder noted that due to the prior design of the space there were lots of small bathrooms, and this was in keeping with there being lots of small single offices. The bathrooms can all be set up as single occupancy, non-gender-specific, and handicap-accessible facilities without it really costing much more. Each could have a handicap toilet stall, a non-handicap stall, and a urinal, as well as a sink. There was quick agreement. Jabar asked for a new set of plans and an updated budget.

Immediately after the meeting, Mai went to see Carlos. "I want to apologize to you about the plans. This is a learning process for me and for the company. We expect to make mistakes. Thank you for being open with me and helping me correct them. We'll probably make more mistakes along the way, but together we can ensure that get things right."

Carlos was happy with the solution and felt reassured by Mai's attitude.

Changing an organization's culture to address the diversity mosaic isn't going to be easy. You must expect that you'll step on a few landmines along the way. When mistakes are made, admit to them, apologize, and move on to a solution. Don't look to develop a track record of instant perfection. Instead, look to do the best you can, be open to criticism, and respond. What matters is where you end up, and that employees and clients can see you were well-intentioned.

Expect resistance.

Amy Bunker
The Lawsuit

It was becoming predictable. Every time a sensitive issue was raised at a leadership meeting, people furtively glanced toward Amy Bunker. A long-time regional sales manager, Amy seemed to take pride in being politically incorrect. Everyone in the industry and the community knew Amy and looked the other way when she made off-color jokes or insensitive remarks. "That's just Amy being Amy" was a common refrain. No one wanted to confront her for fear of escalating the situation. It was exhausting. But the problem was that working with her now was uncomfortable. While some were resigned to biting the bullet for as long as she worked there, others were getting fed up. Angel Rodriguez, the COO, was having a hard time keeping the animosity toward Amy under control, and he knew that Shanelle Lapides, the CEO, simply didn't want to hear about it anymore. She wanted Angel to just make the issue go away. Unfortunately, Angel sensed the issue wouldn't go away until Amy went away.

Angel decided he had to try something. He cleared his calendar and invited Amy out to lunch at a local steak house he knew Amy loved. When she wasn't entertaining clients, Amy was known to have a long, sometimes liquid lunch at the steak house before returning for a leisurely afternoon. After a few minutes of small talk and a drink, Amy, who was no dummy, cut to the heart of the matter.

"Are you trying to fire me or get me to look for a new role elsewhere?" she asked.

"Neither," Angel answered honestly. "I know that sometimes you say things to shock people and reinforce your image. I also know that you have very strong opinions."

Angel said that while he expected Amy to approach the diversity mosaic with open mind, he knew it was unrealistic to expect her to fully embrace it. But he and Shanelle did expect her not to be an obstructionist and not to cause dissent and discord.

"The board is behind the diversity program, Amy. They respect you and all of the programs you have implemented during you time with the company." Angel said that no one wanted to have to choose between Amy and the organization's diversity program . . . because it really wouldn't be a choice. "Please just keep your comments to yourself."

Expect that you'll face resistance. There will be times you are faced with people who will not fully embrace the differences of others because they're ideologically opposed to diversity efforts. There are other times when you'll be faced with people who simply don't understand what diversity means and how it could help the organization, rather than having any ideological opposition to it. If there is any potential for these people to change, wherever their resistance comes from, don't give up on them, but don't let them be a roadblock to your efforts either. Give them an opportunity to be a positive factor, but don't let them be a negative one. Don't expect that they will ever become a supporter. Consider what leverage you have, and what leverage they have, when determining how hard to push for acquiescence. You may have to invest in additional training, and perhaps a coach. The reality is that letting some of these behaviors continue is not an option and you cannot just look the other way. The idea is to work to address the bad behavior, both to end it and to prevent it from spreading.

Do not presume bad intent.

Theresa Stewart
The Saint

It was obvious to everyone on the leadership team that Amy Bunker intended to be an obstructionist. After all, she made her feelings crystal clear. The situation with Max Yorkshire, however, seemed different. Sure, Max was pushing back against many of the organization's efforts, but his objections seemed to be self-centered, not philosophical. There were several people who had pressed Angel Rodriguez, the COO, to confront Max, but Theresa Stewart didn't think that made sense. She had known Max for a long time. She felt he was just wrapped up in himself, as always, angry that others might be receiving helping hands that he had not received himself. She thought it was jealously, not bigotry. She asked Angel if she could speak with Max before any other steps were taken. Angel agreed.

Theresa went to Max's office and got right to the point. "The way you are reacting to our diversity mosaic initiatives is creating the impression among your coworkers that you are biased."

Max seemed stunned. He insisted he wasn't biased and did not have a discriminatory bone in his body. It wasn't that he didn't think people deserved help because of who they are.

"I'm just pissed I never got that kind of help. Why should anyone get help that I never got?" he asked, his temper and voice rising.

Theresa tried to explain to Max that he shouldn't look at things that way. She said that they both had certain built-in advantages that others might not have. She suggested he try not to see the organization's efforts as a way to achieve equality.

"The goal isn't equality," she suggested. "The goal is for us to be a more diverse and inclusive organization, not because that is just, but because that will make us better positioned for the future."

The more they spoke, the calmer Max became. He said he heard what Theresa was saying and was upset that his actions were being misinterpreted. Max said he appreciated Theresa's coming to see him and promised he'd try not to let his frustrations turn into jealousy. Later that day, Theresa went to see Angel and explained that she'd had a good conversation with Max and didn't think anything else needed to be done right now.

It's easy to assume that someone who opposes diversity efforts, or maybe just fails to embrace them, has bad intent, but that assumption does nothing to help and may even exacerbate the situation. Yes, there are people who are biased and who will never come around, like Amy. However, many people simply may not understand or may be wrapped up in a drama of their own, as Max is. Taking the time to talk through the issue, even if it's uncomfortable, could keep someone from being obstructionist, or turn them from being noncommittal to being an ally.

Similarly, don't assume that because someone raises a diversity issue, they are just trying to be difficult or that they are destined to be a problem employee. If an employee asks to leave early to get to a doctor's appointment or to get home in time to see a child's concert, that doesn't mean they're looking to be treated differently. They will be just as supportive of others' needs. The feeling you want to pervade the organization is that we are all in this together, and we all need to respect and look out for each other.

Meet people where they are and celebrate small wins.

Danika Casper
The Wallflower

Danika Casper thought Reese Geller had gone overboard, as usual. Two weeks from now was a Gay Pride festival in the organization's home city. At the prior week's leadership meeting the team had discussed ways the organization could show support. Nothing had been decided, but a few good ideas had been discussed. The plan was to review a list of potential options at this week's leadership meeting and make a final decision as to the best path forward. When the issue was raised, Reese jumped in to say that she had asked one of her graphic artists to create a rainbow version of the organization's logo and then printed T-shirts and bumper stickers for her team. She'd reached out to several LGBTQ employees and to a local organization to show them the design, and they loved it. Reese implied that everyone in company should wear the shirts one day during Pride Week.

Danika was usually quiet at these meetings. She'd been raised to believe that if you don't have anything new to contribute, it was best to remain quiet. That approach could put her at a disadvantage in this team of extroverts, but she'd discovered that when she did say something, everyone listened very closely. Danika knew she'd have to say something now.

In anticipation of the festival, Danika had raised the Pride issue with her own team, expecting it might be an issue. But she was pleasantly surprised that none of the three employees whose reactions she'd worried about raised strong concerns.

"I'm supportive of everyone's rights," said one of her team members, "and don't have a problem with the organization being the same. After all, the organization has supported my needs when it comes to holidays and parties."

The other two team members Danika had been concerned about agreed with those sentiments. Then one of them added, "after all, it's not like you're asking us to stand outside and wave a flag."

Danika knew that asking those three employees to make a public demonstration of their support by wearing a T-shirt or putting a bumper sticker on their car would be pushing them too far. She interrupted Reese's ongoing speech.

"I need to say something."

You could hear a pin drop.

Danika explained the situation of her three employees. She stressed that they were supportive, and certainly would not be obstacles, but that they should not be expected to become public advocates in a way that would make them uncomfortable. Reese suggested that the employees needed to "wake up and embrace diversity." A couple of other members of the team spoke up for Danika's position. When she had a chance to speak again, Danika said that she thought it was important for the organization to meet people where they were.

"These three people are actually trying to be allies. Let's celebrate their support as a win. We're supposed to be about inclusiveness, right?"

Shanelle Lapides, the CEO, responded immediately, putting an end to what might have been a rejoinder from Reese.

"Thank you for your comments, Danika, and for your efforts. Reese, we should publicize our support, but I agree with Danika and don't think we should mandate that employees wear anything which could make them personally uncomfortable. By the way, this is just the kind of discussion we should be having."

We all have the same goal. But not everyone is starting at the same place or is going to evolve at the same pace. Support all movement in the right direction, even if it is not as sweeping as you'd like. Building the diversity mosaic is a marathon, not a sprint.

Look for proactive small-scale changes.

Stacey MacArthur
The General

Stacey MacArthur, who headed up the quality control department, was struck by Danika's notion of accepting small steps as wins. Stacey was always looking for big wins for the organization, judging everything by how it contributed to the core mission. Maybe, Stacey thought, there were some small things that could be done to promote the diversity mosaic that might not be dramatic when taken individually, but could present real progress when taken together. By proactively looking for things that could be improved, potential future problems might be avoided. She also thought that her team, trained to be sticklers for detail, would be perfect for the project. At the next meeting of her direct reports, Stacey asked them to spend some time looking for little things that could be done to promote the organization's initiatives. In keeping with the small-scale theme, she told them she'd give out a homemade mini muffin for each suggestion.

At the next team meeting, one member pulled out a copy of the employee handbook, time sheets, vacation request forms, and expense forms, which she'd covered with yellow Post-its. A skilled editor, the employee had revised the language to be gender- and non-binary inclusive. Jokingly, the employee noted that Stacey would need to bring in two dozen mini muffins because even some of the signs in the office weren't gender-neutral. Laughing, Stacey asked for more ideas. Another employee had scoured the organization's job postings for the past year and reviewed all of the current job descriptions. He'd found that there were at least six instances in which the organization asked for requirements that weren't necessary, and another four instances when there were candidate review guidelines that could be viewed as ageist. He also pointed out that online job postings were limited to sites that focused on affluent, highly educated candidates. Finally, Stacey's administrative assistant passed around a list of all the vendors the organization had used for things like supplies, coffee and snacks, car service, and cleaning. He pointed out that many of the vendors were national or regional companies even though there were local alternatives, many owned by women or minorities. With that, Stacey announced that she'd be bringing three dozen muffins to the next meeting and said anyone with dietary issues could let her know privately and she would work to address them.

Small, proactive steps do more than just potentially avoiding future problems: they help establish a tone and culture. The type of project Stacey put together can help an organization and its employees retrain their brains and learn a new focus and approach. Offering opportunities for employees to get involved in the diversity mosaic process, even if only with small steps, helps make it a more inclusive process. My suggestion when following this strategy is to fol-low what is called the SMART approach: make sure your team's finite proac-tive efforts are specific, measurable, action-oriented, realistic, and time-based. When employees begin to proactively look for differences that may need to be addressed, you can rest assured your organization is on its way toward insti-tutionalizing its diversity mosaic.

You don't need to reinvent the wheel.

Aaron Brady
The Buck Passer

Aaron Brady felt the organization's diver-sity mosaic project was a minefield. He'd seen the difficulties faced by other mem-bers of the leadership team, particularly his friend Davis Orr, who'd been battered by criticism of his efforts to lead the organization's charitable efforts. Aaron had tried to avoid getting involved, but that ended when it came time to begin planning the next year's holiday efforts. Angel Rodriguez, the COO, remembered that Aaron had thought the leadership team shouldn't be involved and should just leave it up to Shanelle Lapides, the CEO. To demonstrate to Aaron that everyone was accountable for creating the organization's diversity mosaic, Angel announced that he and Shanelle wanted Aaron to lead the planning for this year's holiday celebration.

Aaron began by reaching out to various employees about how they felt about last year's holiday plans and prior events. While a handful of staff-ers were happy about not having a party and instead just getting a bonus check, most of the staff felt it had been a cop-out. They missed having a chance to socialize with their coworkers and believed some kind of get-together helped morale. Aaron solicited ideas at the next leadership team meeting. The usual ideas were offered, but it was clear that the team was as frustrated with the issue as he was. Eric Luddy, who had been responsible for arranging the annual client meeting, described what he had gone through and what he and the banquet manager of a hotel had come up with: a combination of a breakfast buffet and a lunch time salad bar. Eric and most of the rest of leadership agreed that the client meeting approach had been successful.

After the meeting, Aaron began thinking that perhaps he could adapt the approach used at the client meeting. The organization could approach the whole day as an event. A breakfast spread could be brought in, followed by a lunchtime salad bar buffet, and then a late afternoon spread of snacks and cocktail party food. There could be a variety of dishes that would provide options for everyone. People could "graze" throughout the day and bring plates back to their offices or the conference rooms if they wished. Staff could be told that it was intended to be a leisurely day rather than the usual fast-paced workday. That would be reinforced by making it a casual dress day as well.

Aaron asked Angel for his notes from last year's meeting and went back over the objections raised around last year's holiday party. Some people thought holding an event during the day made it less festive. Aaron thought by making it a full-day event and having it be a casual dress day too, there would still be a festive spirit. The organization could even put up seasonal decorations—all secular and non-denominational. And, because of the timing, there would be no additional budgetary impact for the unionized staff.

There would be no travel or childcare issues because it would be a workday, and the staff at reception and security could freely take part: They could go to the buffets on their breaks and even bring plates back to their workstations.

When Aaron raised his idea at the next meeting, the response was immediate. The leadership team loved it. Angel liked the idea that people had the flexibility to do essential work and still celebrate. Jamie Little from

HR thought making it a full day that showed appreciation for the staff would be great for morale. And Jabar Pyncher, the CFO, was happy because the total cost of three buffets would still be less than a more formal event. Shanelle said they could even afford to get a little gift for everyone—maybe some form of organization-related swag—and have it available at that late afternoon buffet. Supervisors could also pick up the swag for any of their team members who were unable to pick up the gift on their own.

There's no requirement that every solution be unique even if every problem is unique. If a solution works in one situation, don't shy away from tweaking it to fit other situations. Similar approaches can demonstrate a consistent vision and help create a new culture.

It's never too late to admit mistakes.

Davis Orr
The Defender

Davis Orr was feeling better about being the front person for the organization's charitable efforts. He'd learned from the controversy over his partnering with a restaurant chain that the LGBQT community found problematic. He'd anticipated the problems that would arise if he followed through on his initial plans to partner with a religious charity for the organization's year-end charity drive. After coming up with the solution of working with the local non-profit for the year-end drive, he felt like he was getting ahead of controversies and establishing an equitable, inclusive, and sustainable process for the future. But then he saw the letter to the editor.

For years, the organization held a Halloween party for children of staff and for the entire community. Staff of the organization baked treats, giving it an old-fashioned, homey feel. It was a community fixture for more than a decade until fears of allergies and parental worries about children eating unpackaged treats made it untenable. Rather than turning to a caterer or just serving packaged candy, the organization decided to replace the Halloween party with a fall food drive for those in need.

The local newspaper had decided to run a nostalgic feature article about past traditions in the community. One of the notable traditions featured was the organization's annual Halloween party. The newspaper chose to illustrate the article with a photograph from the 1982 party of the organization's board dressed in costumes, handing out treats to local children. The board had decided to follow a theme: They all dressed like breakfast characters. The board chairman was Tony the Tiger. One member was Captain Crunch. Three other members of the board were Snap, Crackle, and Pop. Taking pride of place in the photo was the then CEO of the organization, dressed like Aunt Jemima, handing out candied apples.

A letter to the editor appeared in the same newspaper a few days after the article ran. It was from a local activist who took the newspaper and the organization to task for racism. The individual said that the costume worn by the former CEO was doubly offensive because of the misogynistic as well as racist trope the Aunt Jemima character represented. The letter writer demanded an apology from the newspaper for running the photo and from the organization for sponsoring the offensive event.

A dejected Davis went to the leadership meeting the next day. Most everyone had read the letter. Amy Bunker snickered, received a glare from Angel Rodriguez the COO, and then said nothing. Jamie Little worried out loud that there would be other old photos reappearing that could now bother people. Asa Lattery suggested the organization not do anything now and wait to see if there were any other letters in the weeks to come. Mai Olaf noted that there was a meme she'd seen that said, "There is no expiration date for disrespect." Jabar Pyncher, the CFO, noted that "apologies don't cost us anything." Sensing where the discussion was going, Davis suggested he work with Mai, the head of marketing, to come up with an apology and submit a letter to the editor.

Later that afternoon, Logan Brita recounted to Davis that lots of companies end up apologizing for things that were done years, decades, and in some cases, centuries ago. She noted that none of the board members in that photo were even alive today.

"Of course, that might not matter to some people. Let's acknowledge it was wrong, say that up until now we weren't aware of the past behavior, apologize for the pain it caused, and say that it doesn't reflect the current attitudes or beliefs of the organization," she suggested.

Mai, Jabar, and Logan are all correct. Taking responsibility for offenses that were not directly engaged in by the current leadership can send a very powerful message. It's generally advisable not to question someone's perceptions or to argue over intentions, and it's never too late to admit a mistake.

Expand your inner circle by dividing projects into smaller pieces.

Waylon Jones
The Brown-Noser

After the team reviewed and approved the apology text developed by Davis Orr and Mai Olaf in response to the organization's historic Halloween mistake, Shanelle Lapides, the CEO, brought up an issue that had been on her mind for months.

"I have a great deal of respect for all of you on this leadership team," she said, "but if the past year has taught us anything, it's that we need to get input from a more diverse group to make sure we're addressing more differences."

She asked for a volunteer to take on the task of coming up with ways to broaden the "inner circle." Ever eager to please, Waylon Jones jumped at the opportunity to take on the boss's latest initiative.

Waylon thought that the best first step in his effort would be to reach out to someone else on the leadership team whom he was close to and who might have more insight into the issue. Over the years, he and Danika Casper had grown close. Waylon knew that most of the leadership team thought of him as a brown-noser and didn't take him seriously. But he and Danika had joined the organization at the same time and had bonded over their shared shyness. His response to his innate shyness had been to become extremely supportive of the CEO. He'd tried to encourage Danika to do likewise, but she had chosen to remain in the background as much as possible. Waylon thought that, as a person of color, Danika might have insights that could help him figure out how to broaden the "inner circle."

Over drinks after work, Waylon told Danika about his initial idea of recruiting an employee who represented each protected class and inviting them to form a diversity team that could be an advisory group to the existing leadership team. Danika listened closely to Waylon's idea and waited for him to finish. When he had, she explained to him that having grown up as a person of color in a primarily white community, she'd often been called on to provide "the minority viewpoint." Initially she'd offered her input, but as time went on, she became more and more resentful about being asked to serve as the, in her words, token person of color. Danika said that she appreciated Waylon's good intentions but added that someone from a protected class should not be required to be the spokesperson for their class.

Waylon was stunned that Danika, who so often was quiet, was so vehement about the situation. He apologized, and asked her what he should do. He explained that he felt caught in a catch-22: he wanted to get diverse input, but now felt that asking people for that diverse input was problematic. Danika said she knew Waylon meant well, and suggested they keep talking about possible solutions. As the evening went on, Waylon came up with the idea of bringing in more and more people. Danika thought about that idea for a moment and said that instead of just expanding the number of people providing input, why not also expand the issues on which those people already provide input?

The lightbulb went on over Waylon's head: "If we divide projects and issues up into smaller pieces, we can pass them on to individual departments and teams. Those groups are already more diverse than the leadership team." Waylon realized that, at the very least, this would provide a larger pool of diverse candidates who might want to participate, and this would also decrease the amount of additional work any individual would be volunteering to do.

"This would help us gain the perspective of all sorts of elements of the diversity mosaic," he noted. Danika agreed.

At the next leadership team meeting, Waylon thanked Danika effusively and presented their idea of dividing diversity initiatives into smaller pieces so they could tap into talent from a greater cross-section of the organization and individuals from protected groups wouldn't feel pressured to volunteer for the initiative or be an organization-wide representative of a protected group. Shanelle loved the idea and urged the leadership team to begin spreading as much decision-making out to as many people in the organization as possible.

Overtly adding people who are different to decision-making groups puts the individuals in a terrible position. They are being asked to serve as a representative of their group rather than as themselves. In effect, they are being reduced to this one element of their identity. Instead of forcing diversity in existing groups, you can divide issues into smaller segments and extend the invitation to participate to new groups across the organization, which presumably will be more likely to possess a wide range of characteristics found within the diversity mosaic. The input of people who are different will be naturally be included without forcing anyone to serve as the sole representative of those who share a particular characteristic.

Work against stereotypes and habits.

Bea Crawford
The Narcissist

Bea Crawford thought about Waylon and Danika's idea of pushing decision-making across the organization. She worried that delegating decisions to her direct reports would result in a lowering of her own profile. But then, later that week, she ran into Shanelle Lapides, the CEO, in the hallway.

"Bea, wasn't Waylon's idea great?" she asked. Without waiting for Bea's answer, she added, "I can't wait to see what all the teams come up with."

Bea realized that she needed to adopt the new approach if she was going to maintain her standing in the organization.

At the next meeting of her own team, Bea brought up the idea. She told the team that she looked forward to bringing them into more decision-making in the future.

"Let's start by throwing open the choice of what movie we should all go to on our next team outing."

Melissa, who'd worked with Bea for almost five years, burst out laughing. Jim and Trey other long standing team members joined in. Puzzled over the laughter, Bea asked what was so funny.

"No offense Bea," Melissa began, "but we've gone to the movies every team outing for the past five years."

Trey added, "I figured you had stock in the movie chain."

Jim said, "Bea, why don't we shake things up and come up with something new to do on the outing, like maybe going out to dinner."

Bea, trying not to feel insulted, agreed. "Okay, I can make reservations for us at The Chowder House."

This time it was Emily, another member of the team, who laughed.

"Okay, what's funny now?" asked Bea, her patience beginning to wear thin.

"Bea, every time the team has gone out to eat in the past three years, we went to The Chowder House. Maybe we can go somewhere else for once?"

Trying to hide her annoyance, Bea agreed, threw open the choice to the team, and agreed to make reservations at Applebee's for their next outing.

When she got home that evening, Bea told her partner Lauren about what had happened. Now it was Lauren who started laughing.

"You too?" Bea asked.

Lauren soothed Bea's feelings.

"One of the things I love about you is that you're so consistent," Lauren said. "But sometimes consistency becomes predictable and predictable becomes a rut."

Bea and Lauren had a long conversation about how working against stereotypes and consciously trying to break habits was good for people's emotional growth and couple's development.

"By the way," Lauren added, "what's good for a couple is probably also good for a team."

At the next meeting of her team, Bea made an announcement.

"First, no laughing," she said with a smile to show she was joking. "I've realized that we've fallen into habits. I want to open up our decision-making as a team by getting everyone to help me break some of these routines."

Bea said that their first decision should be reassessing the day and time and frequency of their team meetings, and whether they should hold them in person or via Zoom. She was amazed at how enthusiastically the team jumped into reviewing each "habit."

When the leadership team came together a week later and Shanelle raised the question of pushing decision making across the organization, Bea jumped into the conversation. She explained what had happened with her team and noted how revisiting stereotypes and habits had really sparked the team.

"And that's why we're not having ham at the holiday party anymore," Angel joked.

Individuals and groups naturally fall into habits. There's usually a good reason for this. When we find something that works, we tend to stick with it. That makes things easier since time and effort doesn't need to be devoted to going over the same issue and reweighing options. The problem is that our habits tend to stagnate while our problems tend to evolve. Over time, what worked stops working and what was once acceptable to all becomes objectionable to some. Efforts at expanding the diversity an organization will accelerate the time in which habits stop being effective. By reexamining solutions and approaches, often with new perspectives, you'll ensure continued effectiveness.

Normalize the discussion of differences and encourage dissent.

Logan Brita
The Tactless

During the open forum portion of the weekly leadership meeting, Jamie Little said she had been surprised by the degree to which conversations and discussions about how the organization should address differences had turned heated.

"We're normally such an easy-going organization," she noted, "and we seemed to have lost some of that in the past year."

Logan Brita and Stacey MacArthur each agreed, and from the common nodding of heads, Angel Rodriguez, the COO, could see the feeling was almost unanimous. Ironically, Logan, who never shied away from disagreements, said she thought they had to do something immediately to fix the situation. Angel, seeing this as a possible professional development opportunity for Logan, asked her to study the issue and get back to the group the following week with solutions.

Initially, Logan thought the best way to handle the issue would be for either Angel or Shanelle Lapides, the CEO, to be stricter in the way they tackled the initiatives. *I'd simply issue orders*, she thought, *and make sure people do what they were told.* While that might have been her preference, Logan knew she couldn't suggest a more aggressive approach. She began doing research on ways to make discussions less forceful. Logan looked for case studies on how other organizations had dealt with similar issues.

She thought that minimizing the number of times differences were discussed would in turn minimize the number of heated conversations. Logan found that while that might indeed decrease the number of angry meetings, it would also increase the intensity of the anger. She read that sociology research showed that the more a controversial issue was discussed, the less controversial it became. It also turned out that her instinct that being more authoritarian would quell controversy was also wrong. Research also showed that encouraging dissent actually helped reduce anger. It was how letting steam escape reduces the pressure and temperature.

At the next leadership meeting, Logan handed out a memo she had prepared. She explained that it suggested the best ways to deescalate the emotions surrounding efforts to expand the organization's diversity mosaic. Logan advised that rather than limiting discussions regarding differences to specific agenda items, it should become one of the regular items on the leadership team's weekly schedule. She also suggested that diversity mosaic reporting become a regular item on the meeting agenda for every group discussion throughout the organization, not just for the leadership team.

"I did some research and the more we and everyone else in the organization discuss differences, the more it becomes a normal and accepted part of our operations," she explained. "Once it becomes a regular discussion, a lot of the heat surrounding these types of discussions should significantly decrease."

Next, Logan moved on to her other point. "I know this sounds out of character for me," she joked, "but I think we need to come up with ways to encourage dissent in the organization."

Pretending not to notice the number of stunned faces in the meeting, Logan explained that her research showed when an organization treats dissent as helpful, not harmful, disagreements become discussions rather than disputes.

"In the same way that we are working to become more comfortable with differences, we also need to become more comfortable with differences of opinion. I'm going to do everything I can to work toward that change in our culture."

It's human nature to become more emotional and strident the less frequent an issue is discussed. That's because the stakes are higher the less often the discussion takes place. Discuss where you're going to go out for dinner every Friday night, and the results of each individual conversation means less than when you go out to dinner once a year on your birthday. You're also more likely to be open to different opinions when you know the stakes of going along with that other opinion are lower since you're going to have the conversation again next week and you will likely have the opportunity to have your own suggestion heard and perhaps acted upon. The more often you discuss differences and the more dissent over differences is not just tolerated but encouraged, the more diversity will become normalized. Debate diversity mosaic decisions once a year and it becomes a major issue for the organization. Address diversity mosaic decisions as an element in every other decision and they're no longer so dramatic because the stakes do not seem as high.

Learn and teach acceptance.

How do I make it work?

Angel Rodriguez
COO

It had been a long year for Angel Rodriguez, the organization's COO. Shanelle Lapides, the CEO, had asked him to take charge of all the organization's efforts to boost diversity, both internally and externally. Angel had delegated management of many projects to members of the leadership team and was mostly pleased with their performance. Some had adapted quickly to the challenges of managing the organization's diversity mosaic, while others had struggled for a time but came up with solutions to problematic situations. He took pride in how Logan became a force for calming discussions. Angel felt the organization had even figured out how to rein in Amy Bunker. There was only one recurring issue he felt still had to be addressed: the attitude of Jabar Pyncher, the organization's CFO.

Jabar isn't consciously biased against anything . . . other than spending money. His penny pinching has been an obstacle to many of the organization's efforts. When adding a new team was proposed, Jabar suggested that the task could be handled by one person. When adding a single staff person was proposed, Jabar asked why new tasks couldn't just be added to the workload of existing personnel. If Jabar could be convinced that there was too much work to add to someone's existing job description, Jabar asked why the organization couldn't hire a part-timer or bring in an independent contractor.

Angel understood that keeping a close eye on spending was part of Jabar's role, and that in some ways he was just doing his job by questioning the cost of every initiative. But Angel and other members of the leadership team had begun to think that there was more to Jabar's resistance than just doing his job. Angel decided the time had come to have a sit-down with Jabar to discuss the issue. To keep the conversation non-confrontational, Angel asked if he could come to Jabar's office, where he knew the CFO would be more comfortable. This would also make it clear that the conversation wasn't a reprimand.

Angel began the discussion with a quick review of the history of the organization's diversity mosaic program and noted Jabar's pattern of responses. Noting that he didn't see anything to suggest Jabar was consciously biased and that his role was to watch spending, Angel asked to what else Jabar attributed his reluctance.

"I don't see the return on investment," Jabar admitted. "We're spending all this time and money doing things that don't seem to directly contribute to the bottom line."

Thanking Jabar for his honesty, Angel explained that neither he, nor Shanelle, nor the board, expected there to be any immediate financial return for these programs.

"We want to do this right," he said. "In the past, organizations like ours didn't need to work with different types of people, but attitudes in our culture, our community, and our industry are changing. It's no longer acceptable. All of us, including you Jabar, need to accept that it is going to take time, and money, and training for us to make things right." He also pointed out that this was a long-term investment because a more diverse organization would be better situated to thrive in the future.

Jabar noted that he heard what Angel was saying, but worried about how high expenses were getting.

"I understand that," Angel said, trying to think of a financial way to frame the issue. "We need to look at this as an investment, not an expense. This is an investment we're making in the long-term viability of the organization and its mission. Think of the organization as being like someone who hasn't invested for their own retirement for a long time, and now has to catch up to compensate for that failure over the years. We have to accept that because we did not make the regular investments in diversity that we should have over the years we have to make larger investments now.

"Besides," he added, "not everything we spend money on has to have a direct return on investment. There are times when we need to spend to do the right thing for our clients, our staff, and the community."

That analogy seemed to do the trick for Jabar. He seemed genuinely to appreciate the situation and resolved not to be as recalcitrant in the future.

"I'm never going to be happy about spending more," he said, "but I think I get it now."

Time invested in understanding the points of view of those you think are resisting diversity mosaic efforts is time well spent. Try to move away from reflexive judgments and knee-jerk reactions and help others to do the same. Differences of opinion are an important and significant element of the diversity mosaic. Accepting another's point of view as valid, even if you disagree, is often enough to get buy-in.

Review your mission statement.

Jessenia Cannon
The Projector

Jessenia Cannon had been thinking about all the efforts the leadership team had been making to embrace differences and use them to improve the organization's culture and solidify its future. She wondered what she could do to help, feeling that she really hadn't contributed as much as she should. One day, when she was walking to the front door from the parking lot, she focused on the company motto etched into the side of the building. It was the statement of purpose from the founder: "We will always try to be and do the best for our clients and for each other." She and everyone in the company saw it almost every day. Maybe, she thought, the organization should develop another statement, this one about differences. She resolved to raise the idea with Jamie Little, the HR director.

Later that afternoon she went to Jamie's office and raised her idea.

"Well, we already add the statement that we're an equal opportunity employer to all our job postings. That's what the lawyers told us we should do." After a few minutes of discussion Jessenia and Jamie agreed that the simple legal statement didn't really seem to match the organization's new culture. Jamie offered to put together a first draft that the two of them could go over at a subsequent meeting.

A week later, Jamie arrived at Jessenia's office and showed her a new statement she'd drafted.

"I reached out to the lawyers, and together this is what we came up with." The new statement read like a laundry list rather than any kind of inspiring message:

> *All our decisions are based on business needs, job requirements, and individual qualifications, without regard to race, color, religion or belief, national, social or ethnic origin, sex (including pregnancy), age, physical, mental or sensory disability, HIV Status, sexual orientation, gender identity and/or*

expression, marital, civil union or domestic partnership sta-
tus, past or present military service, family medical history or
genetic information, familial or parental status, or any other
status protected by the laws or regulations in the locations
where we operate.

Jamie said that the list was so long because she and the lawyers didn't want to leave any group out.

"Maybe we could go in another direction," Jessenia suggested, offering to take a stab at it herself.

That weekend, Jessenia did research on the Internet, looking for various equal opportunity statements. Many took the same laundry list approach Jamie and the lawyers suggested. But a few organizations went in a different direction that Jessenia thought was more meaningful and didn't just seem like fine print. She thought they could keep from leaving a group out by not trying to come up with a list, but by making a simple general statement. By making a positive statement, saying what the organization supported, not just what it opposed, it could be more meaningful.

On Monday, when she returned to work, Jessenia stopped by Jamie's office and read what she had come up with:

"We celebrate diversity and differences and are committed to creating an inclusive and supportive environment for all employees." Jamie thought it was perfect and suggested they bring it to the leadership team at the next meeting.

At that next meeting there was unanimous approval of Jessenia's draft. Shanelle Lapides, the CEO, and Angel Rodriguez, the COO, shared a quick glance and Shanelle nodded.

"Jessenia, Shanelle and I would like you to take on a new initiative for us. We need to draft a diversity mosaic policy. And since you did such a great job with this statement, we'd like you to take the lead on that project. Why don't you and Angel meet later and see what current project you can hand off in order to take this new one on."

* * *

We'll be going over Jessenia's efforts to lead the crafting of the organization's diversity mosaic policy and the lessons it can teach us in the next chapter. But before that, I wanted to provide you with a checklist that summarizes all the methods we've gone over in this chapter.

TAKEAWAYS

- Treating everyone the same can perpetuate issues.
- Equitable treatment can counteract some systemic issues.
- Look for a one-size-fits-all solution while remaining open to some flexibility.
- Delegate the resolution.
- Expect to make mistakes.
- Expect resistance.
- Do not presume bad intent.
- Meet people where they are.
- Celebrate small wins.
- Look for proactive small-scale changes.
- Make sure company language is gender-neutral.
- Review recruiting requirements and sources.
- Review vendor choices.
- You don't need to reinvent the wheel.
- It's never too late to admit mistakes.
- Expand your inner circle.
- Divide projects into smaller pieces.
- Work against stereotypes.
- Normalize the discussion of differences.
- Encourage dissent.
- Learn and teach acceptance.
- Review your mission statement.

CHAPTER 6
PUTTING IT IN WRITING

It is essential that your organization's diversity policies be memorialized in a document so it can be reviewed, revised, and referenced by everyone, from the C-suite to the "shop" floor. To paraphrase the old adage, a verbal diversity mosaic policy isn't worth the paper it's printed on.

I know that policy documents sometimes feel unnecessary. After all, when was the last time you looked at your organization's policy handbook? It was probably when you had a question about vacation days or the organization's medical leave policy. Employees usually don't even know where the handbook is located. Some organizations ensure that all employees receive a printed copy of the handbook. Most, however, inform people that a copy of the handbook is available in some centralized office location or in the HR department's office. Why is it so scarce and hard to find? The cynical say it's to keep employees in the dark about everything to which they're entitled. Actually, I've found that it's usually because the document goes out of date the moment it's printed, and no one wants to take on the chore of collecting old copies and distributing new ones all the time.

Turning the policy statement into an online document that is easily accessible by every employee with Internet access is an obvious solution to making it an organic document. Those employees who don't have work computers or Internet access at home can be given access to the document through shared company computers. If necessary, a handful of copies can be printed and distributed as the exception to the online distribution. If stored on a company site, notifications of any changes can be sent out to the entire workforce using the same communication methods used for other staff-wide announcements. More importantly, the diversity mosaic parts of the document, at least, need to be more than standardized legal text. They need to be regular parts of the organization's management efforts. We can do that by making it a blueprint or agenda with goals and action steps to achieve those goals.

Just think about all the workplace changes brought on by the coronavirus pandemic. An organic diversity mosaic policy can be modified and updated as situations change. And those changes can be disseminated quickly if the policy is primarily an online document.

DEVELOP AN INITIAL LIST OF DIVERSITY GOALS

Start the development of your diversity mosaic policy document by coming up with a list of your organization's diversity mosaic goals. Review all the defensive actions the organization has already taken, if any. What problems or situations led to those actions? Rephrase the problems or situations so they are stated as goals. Remember to use the SMART approach discussed earlier in the book, making sure the goals are specific, measurable, action-oriented, realistic, and time-based. This gives you a quick initial list of the goals that are currently being tackled. But don't leave it there. Explore the factors in your organization that have the greater potential to hinder your efforts and build some additional goals to proactively counteract them.

RISK FACTORS THAT HINDER INCLUSIVITY AND HOW TO TACKLE THEM

As you think of potential challenges to your diversity and inclusion efforts, consider a number of workplace factors that tend to exacerbate those challenges and are breeding grounds for workplace behaviors that will hinder your efforts.[17]

---

17. The Equal Employment Opportunity Commission has an excellent chart, which served as a resource for this section: "Chart of Risk Factors for Harassment and Responsive Strategies," EEOC Public Portal (retrieved from *https://www.eeoc.gov/chart-risk-factors-harassment-and-responsive-strategies* on March 22, 2021).

Are most people in your organization the same? If there are only one or two people in the workforce, in a department, or on a team who are different from the others, they could feel isolated and at risk, or actually be at risk. If the organization, department, or team has a long history of being homogeneous, the addition of new people who are different could make the prior employees feel threatened or uncomfortable and make them prone to saying or doing something that makes new people uncomfortable, or worse. If your organization faces this risk factor, you can list a goal of increasing diversity at all levels of the organization and prescribe action steps for doing that, such as giving reviewing, recruiting, and hiring criteria.

Does your organization have some element of a "locker-room culture"? Some workplaces have an environment that tolerates or even encourages what could be characterized as a "locker-room culture." Typically, these workplaces have been male-dominated, even if not entirely male, and have been known to have a great deal of sexist, racist, and homophobic banter and humor. Employees may claim the culture improves camaraderie and note that even people from protected groups participate in the banter. But that participation may not be voluntary, and those who don't participate in the behavior might be seen as outsiders. If your organization, or part of it, has this kind of culture, your goal should be to create a more civil environment, and your action steps to achieve that can include establishing a code of respect and actively enforcing it.

Does your organization have any new culturally different employees? Employees from other cultures may not be aware of norms in U.S. workplaces that may differ from the norms in other cultures or places. This can result in misunderstandings and even unintentional misbehavior on their part or on the part of others. There might be language barriers that can result in similar issues. Further, employees from other cultures may not know their rights and as a result might be more easily victimized. If your organization has such employees, your goal can be to increase cross-cultural literacy, and your action steps can include providing training to ensure that existing employees understand the cultures of new arrivals and that the new arrivals understand the norms of a U.S. workplace and workforce.

Is there a divisive environment outside your organization? Let's be honest. At the time of this book's writing, every organization faces a divisive

environment outside the workplace. Any talk of what is going on politically outside the workplace can bring anger, disagreement, and harassment into the workplace. Your organization's goal must be to keep the
divisiveness in society from leading to divisiveness inside the workplace.
While the steps you suggest as actions right now should be applicable
to the current situation, do what you can to also ensure that they will
be applicable into the future. For example, assign someone in leadership
to proactively identify events that could lead to a divisive environment.
Don't fixate solely on national or international issues. It's just as likely
that controversial local or regional situations can result in trouble inside
your organization.

Does your organization have a large number of young employees? If you
have a large number of young people in your workforce who are in their
first or second jobs after high school or college, they may not be familiar with accepted workplace behavior and what is illegal. That can lead
them to "misbehave." In some situations, your organization's unique circumstances might make it unlikely you could create a goal of having a
more multigenerational workforce. For instance, the economics of your
operations may mean you primarily attract younger people. Instead, your
goals can be to ensure everyone understands what types of behaviors
are acceptable, and your actions can include providing more or better
training of new hires and supervisors. You can also suggest the development of outreach programs at the local high schools and colleges from
which you draw recruits to discuss appropriate workplace conduct and
expectations.

Are some of your organization's employees valued more than others? Obviously,
organizations have senior managers who play a more significant role than
others. But some organizations also have staff whose key role or high
productivity gives them an actual or perceived higher value than their
peers. A person who services a key client, for example, or a fundraiser
who is particularly productive. Individuals like this may feel like the normal rules don't apply to them, and management may be hesitant to apply
some rules to them for fear of alienating someone very valuable. If this is
the case in your organization, you'll need to have goals to ensure all rules
apply equally. Action steps could include high-level managers proactively
serving as examples by publicly demonstrating their adherence to rules
that some might think wouldn't apply to them. Let's say that everyone

in a department is supposed to take turns cleaning the coffee area. The manager can make a visible show of doing so to make the point clear that the rules apply to everyone.

Are there power disparities in your organization, with the less powerful being overtly different? The larger your organization is and the more layers in your organization's hierarchy, the more power disparities there likely will be between those on the upper levels and those on the lower levels. An organization that has senior executives, professionals, and support staff is different from an organization that has levels from the C-Suite all the way down to the factory floor. The bigger the gap between the upper and lower levels, the more potential there is for low-ranking employees to be exploited, intentionally or unintentionally. And the more those lower ranking employees are comprised of people who are clearly different from the higher-ranking people, the more potentially discriminatory practices could be tolerated. For example, in an organization in which the C-Suite and upper and middle management are primarily men while those working on the shop floor are primarily women, it is more likely there will be sexist or misogynistic behavior. You goal doesn't need to be flattening the organization's hierarchy. It can simply be to ensure rules are applied equally. Your action steps can be similar to those pursued if there are higher value employees: provide training but also look for ways the powerful can demonstrate adherence to the rules.

Does your organization rely on customer satisfaction? When an organization believes the customer is always right or that client satisfaction is the most important goal of the organization, it's possible that inappropriate behavior could be excused if it's what a customer wants. For example, a client shouldn't be given control over whom they work with. A goal in this situation can be to make sure clients or customers aren't being given too much influence. Actions steps can include ensuring that the organization's values take priority over customer satisfaction.

Is your organization's work boring? When employees have a lot of time on their hands because their work is monotonous or repetitive, they may do or say problematic things out of frustration or boredom. Misguided attempts at humor or freewheeling conversations during downtime can result in hard feelings, disputes, or arguments. A goal can be to make work less repetitive. Actions can include forming focus groups and internal task forces to explore work sharing, job restructuring, and other efforts to make work more challenging and interesting.

Is your organization's workplace isolated or decentralized? If your place of business isn't near anything else, employees won't have an opportunity to interact with non-employees. They won't be able to go out for lunch, for example. As a result, employees might begin to get on each other's nerves. Isolated locations can also result in there not being many witnesses to troubling situations or incidents. It's likely not realistic to have a goal of relocating the organization. Instead, consider a goal of making the existing location less isolating for individuals and more flexible. Actions can include providing multiple break rooms, activity areas, and dining areas so people aren't forced into the same location with the same people all the time. Another action can be to make sure there are visible security cameras so there won't be locations where bad behavior can go unobserved. If your organization has a number of locations that separate various levels of the organization, it's possible upper-level supervisors may become out of touch with lower-level supervisors or frontline employees. Lower-level supervisors and frontline employees may not be comfortable or know how to reach out to distant upper-level supervisors. Again, it may be unrealistic to make finding a centralized location a goal. Instead, the goal should be to boost interaction and communications between distant locations. Actions can include having frequent travel between sites and developing clearer lines of communication.

MAKE YOUR POLICY USER-FRIENDLY AND EGALITARIAN

Turning your policy into an online document will certainly make it more organic and accessible, but there's more you can do to make it user-friendly. Rather than using complex legalese or elaborate abstract language, I suggest you craft it as a bulleted outline. By all means, you can start with your organization's mission statement, which—if you followed the guidance from the prior chapter—is simple, direct, and positive. But I would then craft it as a formatted checklist with a brief description of a goal, followed by bullet points describing planned actions. Not only does this type of format make it easier to read, but it also makes it easier to use as a roadmap. Each action can be checked off when it is achieved. If all the actions are completed, the status of the goal can be reexamined. If achieved, it can be checked off as complete. If not, new action steps can be added.

Consider placing the policy in an online location that allows for group input. There are platforms that will allow individual employees to make suggested changes to an online document. Individuals tasked with managing the document receive notifications of these suggestions. The ideas can then be discussed by those charged with defining policies. Another approach is to have a quarterly electronic town hall meeting to discuss suggestions and changes to the policy. The more accessible, user-friendly, and interactive the policy, the more it will be embraced by your entire organization.

Do everything possible to ensure that your policy is crafted with input from every level of the organization, and that when completed, it is perceived as applying to everyone. The C-Suite and rank-and-file employees all need to feel their needs are addressed by the policy. Everyone in your organization should receive training on the new policy. Consider creating multi-level training groups, including individuals from up and down the hierarchy, in each class session. If necessary, encourage upper-level staff to make a conscious effort not to dominate the training session and to encourage full participation from their teams. Your policy needs widespread buy-in to be effective, and people tend to be more supportive of the initiatives to which they contributed. The development of your policy document can't just be a case of going through the motions. It has to be a working plan for the organization's future.

Preparing a Draft Policy Document

Jessenia Cannon
The Projector

Jessenia Cannon hadn't expected to play such a prominent role in the organization's diversity mosaic efforts. Jessenia had jumped into the mission statement project because she'd felt she wasn't pulling her weight in this effort and thought that perhaps others, particularly leadership, might have been feeling the same. It was rewarding to see her efforts on the mission statement recognized. But she was worried now that it was too much recognition. Jessenia thought others would resent her new stature. "Who was she to take on this role?" they'd ask. It was another conversation with Jamie Little, the HR director with whom she worked on the mission statement, that gave her some reassurance.

"You're always concerned with what everyone thinks, so why not use this as a reason to reach out to them?" Jamie suggested.

Jessenia decided Jamie was onto something. But rather than limiting her outreach regarding goals to the leadership team, Jessenia decided to reach out to all levels of the organization. She knew that could become unwieldy, so she came up with a shortcut. Jessenia first set up meetings with members of the leadership team and asked them each to nominate one person from each level of their own hierarchy to serve as a member of a working group.

Jessenia began each discussion with members of the leadership team by asking about recent efforts that were made to expand the organization's diversity mosaic.

- Aaron Brady told her about his experience with the training videos and how he saw the organization could have done a better job hiring outside vendors and consultants that were diverse. (See page 57 to review the whole story.)
- Theresa Stewart explained the lesson she'd learned about understanding that employees have varied economic circumstances and shouldn't be made to feel uncomfortable about their circumstances. (See page 58 to review the whole story.)
- Davis Orr laughed when Jessenia asked him for input. "Everyone remembers what happened to me this past year." Davis said that he'd learned good intentions weren't enough and that the organization needed to make sure it's philanthropic efforts, even in the past, respected differences and that it was never too late to apologize for historic missteps. (See pages 60 and 97 to review the whole story.)
- Jabar Pyncher explained that he'd learned that there needed to be people with different perspectives brought into decision-making and that economic issues couldn't outweigh the need to embrace differences. (See page 117 to review the whole story.)

- Jamie Little told Jessenia that she'd learned not to take people's availability and accessibility to technology for granted. "We can't assume everyone is free to attend events during work hours or can access materials online at home." (See page 70 to review the whole story.)
- Reese Geller seconded Aaron and Jabar's input about getting input from multiple sources, recalling how she'd erred by relying on input just from newer employees when developing external training opportunities. (See page 63 to review the whole story.)
- Asa Lattery laughed when Jessenia described all the others who'd spoken about getting more input. "I learned that too when I worked on coming up with a new dress code." (See page 65 to review the whole story.) "And then I realized how even masks could become divisive issues if we didn't come up with a policy that brought people together." (See page 71 to review the whole story.)
- Shanelle Lapides recounted her experience with assuming that everyone would love the idea of attending baseball games. "You know what they say about what happens when you assume," she joked. (See page 66 to review the whole story.) Shanelle said she'd also made the mistake of assuming people didn't have health concerns about coming back to the office if issues weren't already known by the organization. (See page 73 to review the whole story.)
- Angel Rodriguez thought for a few moments before responding to Jessenia. He said that there were a couple of efforts he'd led that might help. Angel spoke about the need to understand the differences of people with varied family situations (see page 67 to review the whole story) and different ways of commuting to and from work (see page 70 to review the whole story). "I think it's important to realize that embracing differences means paying attention to big issues, like family, but also to things we wouldn't normally think of, like how we get to and from work."
- Max Yorkshire backed up everything others had told Jessenia about the need to get more perspectives involved in decision-making. But rather than leaving it there, Max, whom Jessenia had never seen be an impassioned advocate, spoke to her about how important it was for people who felt that they were somewhat different to have their feelings acknowledged and considered by the organization. "People don't always need to see things decided their way," Max said, "but they need to feel like they're being heard and taken seriously." (See page 102 to review the whole story.)

When Jessenia had finished interviewing the members of the leadership team, she made individual appointments with those from other levels of the organization who had been nominated to serve on her diversity mosaic policy working group to determine whether they would be willing to participate. In addition, the leadership team agreed that in the future, they would look to expand the committee and designate a certain number of spots for self-nominations, as a way to include individuals who may not have been nominated but still had an interest in participating.

With all of her initial interviews complete, Jessenia developed a draft list of goals based on everything she'd learned. She, Shanelle, Angel, and Jamie had agreed that the best approach would be to come up with a draft list of goals, have the working group review the goals, refine the list, and then reconvene the entire working group to work on action steps to address each goal.

"The last thing we want," Angel noted, "is to talk about getting lots of perspectives, and then deliver prescriptions without widespread input."

Shanelle said she'd told Jabar that the organization would foot the bill for an all-day seminar for the working group.

"Just make sure you talk to Eric and Aaron about setting up one of those all-day meetings," he said with a chuckle. "They've become experts."

* * *

On some level, whether Amy Bunker suddenly joins the 21st century or moves onto a new role, or Jabar Pyncher stops being a penny pincher, or any of the other cast of characters in the organization dramatically modifies their personalities doesn't really matter. We are all human beings, with traits, quirks, foibles—and differences—that make us unique. Human beings are frustrating but also fascinating, idiosyncratic as well as inspiring. You'll always need truth vision to understand what they're thinking and feeling. What matters isn't that people's personalities change—that's not going to happen—but that their behavior and the *organization's* behavior changes.

Workplace cultural changes may be dictated from the top down, but they take effect from the bottom up. By regularly stressing that diversity is a mosaic that impacts everyone, constantly looking for ways to push for fairness rather than just equality, and always adopting policies, strategies, and procedures to make diversity a regular part of the organization, you create an organizational habit. Eventually it will become second nature for everyone in the organization to broaden their perspective. There will be a time when there won't need to be both parents and non-parents involved in a discussion about scheduling time off. There will be a time when there won't need to be a vegan as part of the team planning the client conference. There will be a time when the viewpoints and needs of every protected class of people, both inside and outside the organization, will be addressed by a group that doesn't necessarily include them. We will all be allies, looking out for each other's interests. The organization will embrace the diversity mosaic, not as a finite project, but as a constantly evolving approach to business. That is what we are all working toward, and what this book has been all about.

TAKEAWAYS

- Turn the policy statement into a living, breathing document that can be a regular part of the organization's management efforts.
- Construct the document as a set of goals with simple action steps to meet each goal so it becomes a blueprint or agenda that can be easily followed and revised.
- Begin by developing a list of diversity mosaic goals.
- Review all defensive actions the organization has taken regarding diversity. These can be the basis of a list of current goals.
- Explore existing risk factors in the organization to develop further goals.
  - Are most people in your organization the same?
  - Does your organization have some element of a "locker-room" culture?
  - Does your organization have any new culturally different employees?
  - Is there a divisive environment outside your organization?
  - Does your organization have a large number of young employees?
  - Are some of your organization's employees more valued than others?
  - Are there power disparities in your organization, with the less powerful being overtly different?

- Does your organization rely on customer satisfaction?
- Is your organization's work boring?
- Is your organization's workplace isolated or decentralized?

- After developing a draft list of goals, work with a representative cross section of the organization to finalize the list and develop action steps for each goal.

- Consider seeking consistent feedback about updates so that this becomes a regular part of your business operations, as opposed to a daunting task that occurs every few years.

APPENDIX 1

THE LEGAL ISSUES

Protecting your organization from legal liability due to discriminatory policies is an additional benefit to expanding the diversity of your organization, not the primary reason for the effort. Still, there's no getting around it: organizations are prohibited from discriminating based on several different protected characteristics. In practical terms, this means if you look around your workplace and see groups of individuals who all look the same, this could subject your company to significant legal liability if you are intentionally, or even unintentionally, eliminating diverse candidates from consideration. This obligation to refrain from considering certain characteristics when making employment decisions is not limited to hiring decisions, but also extends to decisions related to the rewarding and promoting of employees, and basically to anything involved with the operations of the organization.

I recommend that all employees receive some type of training in legal basics. And I've found that it's often more effective for a well-trained manager to lead this conversation, because a legal presence in a room or on a call can inhibit the kind of frank back and forth that might be required. By reading this book, you now know the types of concerns your employees may have when they learn of these obligations, and you'll be prepared to respond to them. Of course, if at some point you need a legal opinion, you can always consult your attorney or corporate counsel for further guidance, but when it comes to explaining what you and your team need to do and how you need to do it, this is better coming from you. Because this information can be very dry, I like to present it as an FAQ, logically leading the people through the subject.

Q: What are the laws we're talking about?

A: There are four federal laws that have the most significant impact on diversity in the workplace. I'm focusing on these federal laws because they will impact everyone who is reading this book.

- Title VII prohibits employment discrimination based on race, color, religion, sex, national origin, and genetics.
- The Equal Pay Act (EPA) prohibits unequal compensation for men and women who perform substantially equal work in the same establishment.
- The Age Discrimination in Employment Act (ADEA) prohibits discrimination against individuals who are 40 years old or older.
- The Americans with Disabilities Act (ADA) prohibits discrimination against qualified individuals with disabilities.

There are also state, city, and local laws, and even company handbook policies that apply to workplace discrimination. You can generally assume that these additional sources of regulations provide greater employee protections because they expand on the higher authorities' regulations. For example, Title VII applies to employers with fifteen or more employees, New York State anti-discrimination laws apply to employers with four or more employees, and the local laws of a progressive city in New York State may extend coverage to employers of more than two employees.

Q: To what areas of employment do the laws apply?

A: The laws make it illegal to discriminate from advertising and filling a position through the recruitment, interviewing, and hiring of someone, and then including all of the terms and conditions of their employment. The phrase "terms and conditions of employment" has historically been broadly interpreted. Here's a list of some of the commonly understood terms and conditions of employment:

- Recruiting;
- Hiring;
- Compensation;
- Allocation of fringe benefits;

- Testing;
- Training and apprenticeship programs;
- Work assignments;
- Classification of employees;
- Transfers, promotions, layoffs, or recalls;
- Job postings;
- Use of company facilities;
- Retirement benefits;
- Disability leave; and
- Firing.

Q: Who do the laws protect?

A: For an individual to be protected by these laws, they must fall into what is called a "protected class." A protected class is a group of people who share a common characteristic that entitles them to protection for discriminatory and harassing conduct under the anti-discrimination laws we've discussed.

People can belong to more than one protected class. For instance, an African American woman could assert a claim based on both sex and race. A 50-year-old Muslim man could assert a claim based on sex, age and religion. A disabled, gay Asian woman could assert a claim based on any or all of the four protected classes to which she belongs.

And, as discussed above, a state, city, or employer could decide to expand the protections individuals receive under federal law. They do this by prohibiting discrimination based upon a wide range of protected classes that are not protected under federal law. You will have to check with the relevant state and city legislatures as well as your company handbook to find out what specific characteristics are protected in your organization, but the chart on page 138 shows the protected class in three different states to give you a sense of the wide range of characteristics that are protected.

In other situations, a state may decide to protect a characteristic when the issue is raised on a federal level and the deciding authority disagrees with the result. For example, while it is illegal to discriminate based on a feature associated with a racial group, the U.S. Supreme Court has ruled that hair is a cultural rather than racial characteristic. That means discrimination based on hairstyle is not illegal under federal law.

Protected Class[*]	New York	Oregon	California
Age	✓	✓	✓
AIDS/HIV status			✓
Ancestry			✓
Citizenship status			✓
Color	✓	✓	✓
Creed	✓		
Disability	✓		✓
Domestic violence victim status	✓		
Domestic violence, assault, or stalking victim status			✓
Garnishments		✓	
Gender identity		✓	
Gender identity or expression	✓		✓
Genetic information			✓
Familial status	✓	✓	
Marital status	✓	✓	✓
Medical conditions			✓
Mental or physical disability		✓	
Military status	✓		✓
National origin	✓	✓	✓
Opposition to a health or safety condition		✓	
Political activities or affiliation			✓
Predisposing genetic characteristics	✓		
Pregnancy-related condition	✓		
Prior arrest or conviction record	✓		
Race	✓	✓	✓
Religion		✓	✓
Retaliation for opposing unlawful discriminatory practices	✓		
Service in the legislature		✓	
Sex	✓	✓	✓
Sexual orientation	✓	✓	✓
Testimony in employment department hearings		✓	
Use of a protected leave		✓	
Use of tobacco products while off duty		✓	
Veteran's status		✓	✓

[*] *See generally*, "Discrimination – Employment Laws," National Conference of State Legislatures (retrieved from *https://www.ncsl.org/research/labor-and-employment/discrimination-employment.aspx* on March 23, 2021).

New York State strongly disagreed with this decision and subsequently amended its ban on racial discrimination to include traits historically associated with race, including hair texture and protective hairstyles including braids, locks, and twists.

Q: What kind of actions are considered discriminatory?

A: For an individual to have a viable legal claim, they must have been subject to what is called an "adverse action." That means something bad must have happened to them. There must have been an employment decision that had a negative impact on their working conditions.

Adverse action is another phrase that has been broadly interpreted. Here are some common adverse actions:

- Not being hired;
- Not being trained;
- Being offered lower compensation;
- Not being sent to a conference;
- Being denied a vacation request;
- Being reassigned to different responsibilities;
- Being transferred;
- Not being given a raise;
- Not being promoted;
- Being laid off; or
- Being terminated.

Q: Does it matter that we didn't intend to discriminate?

A: No. The intent of an employer isn't relevant to whether discrimination took place. The law recognizes two types of discrimination: disparate treatment and disparate impact. Disparate treatment happens when the intent of the person or policy is to discriminate—for example, a manager who will not hire a woman for a role or a company policy that says only someone born in the United States can be hired for a role. Disparate impact happens when there is no intent to discriminate, but what appears to be a neutral action or an organization's neutral policy results in a disproportionate impact on individuals who are members of a protected class—for example, a manager who will only hire someone with a very active social media profile is likely disproportionately impacting people over 40. A company policy that says it will only hire people with a credit score of 750 or higher is likely disproportionately impacting certain protected groups that historically have lower credit scores.

Q: What if there's a good reason for a policy that might have disparate impact?

A: If there is a good business reason for a policy and there is no lesser alternative to it, the law may not consider it discriminatory even if it has a disparate impact. Let's say the role in question requires an employee to be able to lift and load sacks that weigh 100 pounds. There is no lesser alternative, such as having a second person readily available. This requirement may have a disparate impact on female job applicants. However, because there is a clear business need for the requirement and there is no lesser alternative available, the law will likely not regard it as unintentional discrimination.

APPENDIX 2

SAMPLE DIVERSITY MOSAIC PLAN

Mission: Celebrate diversity and differences and commit to creating an inclusive and supportive environment for all employees.

Goal: To increase the diversity of its workforce by ten percent in the next year.

- **Action:** We will expand our recruiting sources to include those that would provide more diverse candidates, such as the local community college.
- **Action:** We will review all job postings and job descriptions to ensure that they do not contain unnecessary requirements that have the potential to unintentionally disqualify qualified diverse candidates.
- **Action:** We will expand the positive trait list of candidates to include providing a different or underrepresented perspective in the organization or department.

Goal: To make our working procedures and workplace more inclusive to individuals and families of all types and structures.

- **Action:** We will create standing and ad hoc task forces made up of diverse employees from all levels to provide input on recurring and singular issues.
- **Action:** We will create a virtual diversity mosaic "suggestion box" on the organization's SharePoint site to allow for anonymous posting of suggestions, concerns, and comments by all employees.

- **Action:** We will make diversity mosaic updates a regular element in all leadership and team meetings, and we will hold a quarterly all-hands diversity summit discussion.

Goal: To expand our use of diverse vendors, suppliers, and contractors.

- **Action:** We will reach out to the local minority small business associations to find new potential vendors owned and operated by underrepresented groups.
- **Action:** We will reach out to national contractor associations to find new potential diverse contractors.
- **Action:** We will reach out to existing diverse vendors, suppliers, and contractors for references to other diverse vendors, suppliers, and contractors.

Goal: To make our working environment more welcoming and inclusive.

- **Action:** We will adopt an employee-choice PTO policy, allowing individuals to select which days they would like to take off rather than having a set list of company holidays.
- **Action:** We will ensure that every company-organized meal will either consist of employee-provided dishes or be a vegetarian buffet.
- **Action:** We will review all company signage, documentation, and manuals to ensure they do not contain potentially divisive language.

BONUS MATERIALS

Having read this entire book, you know that I believe that expanding our definition of diversity to include all the differences that make up the diversity mosaic is the best way to get employees to shift from opposition and grudging acquiescence to full-throated support. One of the things that has struck me in the past few years as I've been putting forward this approach, is that the difference that gets the least attention is age. You might find it hard to believe, but in my experience more people are willing to address family structure, for example, than they are age, even though the latter is specifically protected by federal law.

The widespread reluctance to address ageism is ironic, since every one of us will get older if we remain alive. No matter your race, gender, sexual orientation, or any other difference, everyone eventually becomes potentially subject to age discrimination. That's why I think the advice about countering ageism that I offered in my book *Over the Hill but Not the Cliff* is more relevant than ever. Here's an excerpt from that book that, I hope, gives those who fear they are subject to ageism guidance on how to overcome this still accepted form of discrimination.

OVER THE HILL BUT NOT THE CLIFF

5 Strategies for 40+ Job Seekers to Push Past Ageism & Find a Job in the Loyalty-Free Workplace

LORI B. RASSAS

Part of *The Perpetual Paycheck* series

INTRODUCTION

AGEISM IN THE
LOYALTY-FREE WORKPLACE

If you find yourself reading this book, you probably have worked for a number of years (or perhaps a number of decades) and plan on working for a number more. If you were to look back at your employment history, I am sure there were high points, when you achieved great success, and times when you were off track. You may have been passed over for a promotion, or not received a job offer after a few rounds of interviews. Perhaps you were laid off through no fault of your own, were terminated for behavior you now regret, made a lateral move, accepted a pay cut to take your career in a new direction, or took a leave of absence to tend to a personal matter. The life events that could have impacted your career are numerous, but like everyone else, your career trajectory includes a number of hills, roadblocks, valleys, bumps, or whichever metaphor best applies. And since you are reading this book, I would also assume you are ready to make a change—or perhaps being forced to make a change.

Now, if you asked me to describe the candidate most likely to find the best new position in the shortest period of time, would that person be an older candidate? Probably not. Then again, it would not be a recent college graduate, a candidate looking to move to a new geographic location, or someone looking to take their career in a new direction and work in a new industry.

No matter what your age or where you are in your career, you will face obstacles. Like death and taxes, they are inevitable. And, as you overcome one challenge (such as a recent college graduate struggling to get a few years of work experience under her belt), another one will surface (such as when that same person decides to move across the country when her fiancé is accepted to medical school there). You just need to identify the specific obstacles that impede your path and work your way past them.

Just as we will all face some obstacles in our career trajectories, all of us will also age—and there will likely be times when our qualifications are overshadowed by our age (and, more to the point, how hiring managers perceive our age). Fair or not, this happens one way or another in virtually every industry. When it happens, we are faced with two choices: We can see it as a cliff and rail against the system, or we can see it as just another hill to navigate along our workplace journey. The good news is that once you climb this hill, there is nothing to stop you from gaining speed and achieving levels of success you did not previously even contemplate.

I can appreciate the fact that ageism in the workplace is a hot-button issue. Break it down to its essence, however, and it is simply no different than any other career obstacle you need to overcome. Once you identify the challenges faced by older candidates, you will be in a better position to scale that hill and move on to the next challenge.

> "Just remember, when you're over the hill, you begin to pick up speed."
> CHARLES M. SCHULZ

If you have picked up this book, you are well on your way to acquiring some incredibly effective tools that will enable you to move up and over this hill. I know you may be frustrated, perhaps because you have responded to at least fifty ads for job openings, reached out to ten people for informational interviews, and scheduled a handful of meetings or job interviews. Despite all your efforts, you have yet to receive a job offer. Or maybe you have worked in the same job for a number of years, have continued to be passed over for promotional opportunities, and are concerned that it is just a matter of time before you are laid off. Or you might be changing jobs in the middle of your career, or you might be out of work for a reason that is no fault of your own.

Whichever scenario fits you best, I am fairly certain you have a very strong work ethic and are committed to remaining in the workforce. But I will also bet that you are having trouble fully committing to a robust job search because it seems like forever since your efforts produced any meaningful results. You might even think your age is the very thing that is holding you back.

If any of the above situations apply to you, even remotely, this is the book for you. I have spent a lot of time navigating the modern workplace and determining the best approaches with the greatest chances of success. This is my business: I am an employment attorney, human resources consultant, career coach, and negotiator. I provide guidance to executives, entertainment personalities, and working professionals at all stages of their careers. Plus, I have sat on the other side of the desk and have represented employers, so I understand how the workplace works from both sides. And, through this work, I have discovered a number of strategies that have enabled older job seekers to use their age—and all of the wisdom, skills, and experience that come with it—to their advantage to achieve unprecedented success.

The loyalty-free workplace is yours to conquer. With some basic knowledge about today's environment, and some new strategies designed to help you tackle it, before long you will find that hill behind you and a new horizon before you.

So, since we aren't getting any younger, it is time to get to work.

YOU CANNOT BE BLAMED FOR HOW OLD YOU ARE

As we move forward, understand one thing: If anyone is to blame for any negative perceptions related to age, it is certainly not you. The fact is, negativity associated with age is ingrained in our culture. Think of the billions of dollars we spend every year on beauty products and procedures designed to prevent or hide the signs of aging. The message is clear: Aging is something we should work to avoid.

The problem, of course, is that all of these products and procedures are built on a fallacy, because all of us are still going to age. As George Carlin once put it, "It's on our schedule."

And these negative perceptions should not come as a shock to any of us since we face them not just as we grow older but from a very young age.

©Glasbergen
glasbergen.com

— GLASBERGEN

"My teacher says little girls can grow up to be anything they choose!
Why did you choose to be an old lady?"

Consider how a child responds when a parent or grandparent makes an innocuous remark like "Oh, boy, I am getting old!" Does the little one say, "Yes, Grandma, you certainly are"? Of course not! Most children (or most anyone else, for that matter) are more likely to say the opposite: "You are *not* old!" or "No, you're not!"

Nevertheless, the message gets conveyed: young = good, old = bad. So, as you grow older, both in general and in terms of your career, do not be surprised if one day (1) you find yourself on the receiving end of some negativity related to your age, or (2) you have to engage in some strategic work to convince someone (such as a hiring manager) that none of the negative stereotypes related to age apply to you.

> "It's paradoxical that the idea of living a long life appeals to everyone, but the idea of getting old doesn't appeal to anyone."
> ANDY ROONEY

NOW, SOME GOOD NEWS

First and foremost, you are not alone. Each day, more than ten thousand baby boomers celebrate their sixty-fifth birthday, and this is expected to continue for decades to come. This well-publicized statistic means that there are tens of thousands of others in their forties, fifties, and early sixties who are right behind them. And not only are people aging, but many members of this vast population are looking for work. Some are unemployed through no fault of their own. Some are currently employed and looking for a change. Some are employed but are concerned that they will not be included in their company's future plans.

No matter what the circumstances, few of these candidates are ready to retire, and many are concerned about their financial future. Some are apprehensive about looking for a new job. Many are angry and frustrated because they believe that rampant age discrimination is the reason for their current situation.

In addition, many older job candidates tell me they are nervous about the process because they have not sent out a cover letter, updated a resume, attended a networking event, or gone on an interview in years (or, in many cases, decades). Some even feel out of their element because this is one of the first times in their working life, if not *the* first time, that they have ever been out of work or felt that their job was at risk.

No doubt, this is daunting—and I certainly empathize whenever I hear a client share a similar experience. At the same time, I cannot help but commend the candidate for being able to tell their story. Why? Because the truth is, very few people who are just now entering today's marketplace will have the luxury of a career that gives them a sense of security for decades. In the loyalty-free workplace, where short-term commitments are the norm and jobs can end at any given time, most people will find themselves continuously engaged in the job search. Few expect to be in the same position for more than five years, let alone work in the same position or even with the same company until their fifties or sixties. So, in this regard, if you are embarking on your first true job search, or if you are back in the job market for the first time in thirty years, this is actually quite an accomplishment, for which you should be very proud.

PREPARE FOR THE WORST AND EXPECT THE BEST

For an older candidate starting to develop a job-search strategy, the best approach is to think of the development of an age-specific job search as the umbrella you tuck in your bag on a sunny day. It is not that you do not trust that the sun will continue to shine; you just want to be prepared if and when the storm hits.

This is the best strategic approach, because we may never know if our application was turned down, or if we did not get an offer after interviewing, because of our age. Nevertheless, we still have to approach the job-search process knowing that it *may* happen. This is no different than many other decisions we make in our lives. We purchase health insurance even though many of us may never need a major surgery. We purchase homeowner's insurance even though, thankfully, most of us will never be faced with the total loss of our home. However, just the possibility of its occurrence should motivate us to prepare for it.

Practically speaking, how do we do this? By casting a very wide net. After all, even if age discrimination is one reason why you are not getting the job offers and opportunities you deserve, it might not be the only one.

EMBRACE THE AGING PROCESS

Consider this: You wake up in the morning, swing your legs off the bed and stand up. Few people upon waking spend any time wondering whether their feet will hit the floor. Why? Because when you open your eyes, you know gravity is there, so you do not spend any precious time thinking about it.

This analogy applies to older candidates and their job-search process in two important ways. We can wake up each morning and worry about whether we will age. However, just like gravity is a constant, so is aging. Ten years from now, we will be ten years older than we are today. Whether we think about it or not, it will happen.

> "If you're always battling against getting older, you're always going to be unhappy, because it is going to happen anyhow."
> MITCH ALBOM

I have a relative who, in her late thirties, told our family that she had been accepted into medical school and was going to become a doctor. We were all taken aback at this decision, especially since she had already achieved career success in an unrelated field. In fact, one family member said, "Wow, that seems so depressing—she will be middle-aged and just starting out as a doctor." Almost instinctively, I replied, "There is no avoiding the fact that in ten years she will be middle-aged. So she might as well be a middle-aged doctor."

My point is that rather than spending our time, energy, and resources thinking about whether we are going to age, why not focus instead on something we can control: how to prevent the aging process from disrupting our stream of income.

YOUR AGE CANNOT HURT YOU, BUT LYING ABOUT IT WILL

Many of the strategies we will discuss relate to changing the way hiring managers perceive our age. This is quite different from lying about our age or trying to convince a hiring manager we graduated from college during the millennium when it was actually two or three decades before.

> Overheard:
> *Husband:* Does this outfit make me look younger?
> *Wife:* No, the outfit makes you look like a seventy-five-year-old in Lycra shorts.

It makes no sense to hide your age, because you can only hide it for so long. Even if you completely sanitized your resume, removing any evidence of the generation you associate with, at some point you will be sitting in front of a hiring manager who will see through your deception. While some employment experts say that once an older candidate gets that far in the process, their age is a nonissue, most hiring managers will beg to differ. After all, if you lied about your age just to get an interview, who is to say what else you have lied about and what else you will lie about if you get the job?

The idea that gravity, just like the aging process, will continue to exist also relates to the discussion of ageism in the workplace. I have seen it countless times through the experiences of my clients, colleagues, and some very close friends. Consider the social experiment set up by the AARP (the American Association of Retired People) (video of this experience is available at *http://www.aarp.org/disrupt-aging/stories/ideas/info-2016/ no-donuts-for-you-video.html*). This experiment involved a food truck with a prominently displayed sign that read "No One Over 40 Years of Age Will Be Served." As paying customers approached, a salesperson turned away customers who were clearly older than forty, saying simply that the company "did not believe they were the right fit for their business," while telling those customers who were under forty that they had "exactly the vibe they were looking for." The responses varied. Some people accepted the conditions, while others said it was ridiculous. One person insisted that she wanted to buy the decadent treats not for herself but for her daughter—at which point, the salesperson said she would sell her the treats if the woman promised she would not eat them herself (and that she would step away from the truck as she waited for them to be prepared). The absurdity of this condition was not lost on anyone who witnessed the scene. Yet, this is precisely what is happening in our workplace. Every. Single. Day.

Age discrimination is real. It is present. It is illegal. It is wrong. The problem, however, is that unlike in the very telling AARP experiment, the signs of discrimination are not as blatant, and neither is the connection between the adverse event and the person's age. In many cases, discrimination happens outside the public's view, and even when it occurs more openly, it is difficult to prove. This reality makes it less likely for a victim to invest the time, energy, and resources to pursue it.

From a practical standpoint, there are other reasons why you may not want to voice your concern that a company is engaging in discrimination. For one, employers are overwhelmed with candidates and looking for reasons to exclude them; you do not want to make that decision any easier for them than it should be. Employers also hire cautiously, hoping to minimize the chances that they will bring a candidate with a negative attitude, or someone who is angry, into the workforce. This is why I encourage clients to be positive and supportive of prospective employers, rather than confrontational and critical. After all, your main focus is to find a job that offers the stream of income you need to provide for yourself and your family.

Many of us may feel that "we know it when we see it," and if you are personally impacted by age discrimination, you may be angry and frustrated. However, if your goal is to find a job, when you are faced with this type of situation, the best response is to redirect your time, money, and energy toward employers who are less likely to engage in it (or hire you in spite of it).

This is not to minimize the importance of working to eradicate age discrimination and compel compliance with the law. But if your goal is to navigate the loyalty-free workplace successfully as an older employee, your best strategic move in terms of your job search is to be aware of the signals of potential age discrimination and work around them.

AGE IS NOT ALWAYS A FACTOR

Another reason not to blame ageism for why you are stuck in your job search is that, in some cases, it might not be the only reason for your situation. Or it may not have anything to do with your current situation.

> Account executive Davis Hocker, 56, is laid off after his company closed the satellite office where he had been working for close to three decades. Davis has been looking for a new opportunity for six months and has yet to receive an interview. During that time, he sent out over one hundred cover letters and resumes, hearing back from only eighteen prospective employers, who informed him that a more suitable candidate had been selected for the position. Davis concludes that age discrimination will prevent him from re-entering the workforce.

Davis' situation is all too common. But without further information, it is virtually impossible to determine whether his inability to land a new opportunity is strictly due to his age. For all we know, there may be other forces at work. Sometimes, a hiring manager will reject a candidate because he did not follow directions in the application process or sent in a poorly formatted resume. If one or both of these are true, Davis should be able to quickly and effectively address these issues and secure a new position. (We will be discussing some ways older candidates can make their resume work best in Strategy #1 and its appendix.)

Even if you were eliminated from consideration due to your age, do not automatically assume that the result would have been any different if you had been younger. Perhaps you interviewed poorly because you have not looked for a job in quite some time and were therefore out of practice. Perhaps you are relying on job-search techniques that worked well in the 90s but are no longer effective based on the realities of the loyalty-free workplace. Perhaps the prospective employer spoke with one of your references and they gave you a less-than-glowing recommendation. Perhaps you have the precise experience to fulfill the position, but the candidate who was hired had experience that was off the charts. Or maybe you were one of two finalists but lost out to the other candidate because she had a long-established personal relationship with one of the company's larger clients.

The fact is that any number of factors goes into a company's decision to hire a particular candidate. You may never know the true motivation for why they did not choose you.

Not only that, but even if your age *was* a factor, no hiring manager will ever tell you that—unless they want to subject themselves and the company to a legal discrimination claim.

The fact is that ageism may or may not play a role in a decision that results in your not getting the job offer. So, the question becomes, how do you properly prepare for this uncertainty? By using strategies that will overcome ageism if it plays a role but will not detract from your success in the event it does not.

"DRESSING" FOR SUCCESS

Imagine you hired a Hollywood stylist to help you become camera-ready for your walk down a red carpet. Naturally, you would want her to know all the basics to make you look fabulous on the big night. This includes the most appropriate fabrics and styles based on current trends, as well as whether it is a day or an evening event, the season, and the expected weather. Once the stylist gathers all of that information, she will use them as building blocks to create an age-appropriate outfit. After all, two people going to the same event (even if they are the exact same size, and have the exact same coloring) may be dressed completely different according to their age.

This is precisely how I approach the job-search advice you will find in this book. Our discussions about overcoming how prospective employers see your age will be tailored to a job search in the loyalty-free workplace. This, after all, is the employment environment we are all dealing with right now, so any effective strategies must take this into account. Once this foundation is laid, we will modify these strategies to ensure they address some of the biggest challenges faced by job seekers of an advanced age. Just like the Hollywood stylist, I want to be sure you possess not just *any* tools to survive in the loyalty-free workplace, but the *age-appropriate* tools that will enable you to truly thrive.

IT IS NEVER TOO LATE TO TAKE YOUR FIRST STEP

One other thing to keep in mind: No matter what your age, or where you are in your career or job-search process, you can do this. It is never too soon or too late to modify your strategies to achieve the greatest amount of success.

Financial advisors always emphasize the importance of starting to save for retirement at the earliest age possible. If you start saving in your twenties, you will increase the chances of achieving financial security during your retirement years. Even if you never thought about saving for retirement until you were fifty-five or sixty-five, it is not as if the advisor will say, "Sorry, too late, there is nothing I can do for you." More likely, the advisor will work with you so that you can make the best choices from this point forward. Since giving up on your job search is not an option, the only way to turn your fortunes around is to make a change today.

Before you start to limit your goals based on your late start, keep in mind that countless others have achieved great success later in life. Vera Wang did not start designing wedding dresses until she was forty. At fifty-seven, Chesley "Sully" Sullenberger III landed US Airways Flight 1549 in the Hudson River, saving the 155 passengers aboard; and at sixty-five, Colonel Harland Sanders started the KFC franchise. Ronald Reagan was fifty-five when he was elected to his first political office, and he became president at the age of sixty-nine, just a few weeks before his seventieth birthday. Even President Reagan was outdone by Nelson Mandela, who was seventy-six when he became president of South Africa.

> "It is a mistake to regard age as a downhill grade toward dissolution. The reverse is true. As one grows older, one climbs with surprising strides."
> GEORGE SAND

In addition, in a number of ways, the dynamics of the loyalty-free workplace actually favor older candidates. That may seem hard to believe at first, but once you understand the differences between the modern workplace and how things used to be, you will see a number of advantages that you will want to eagerly exploit.

COMPANIES COURT COMMITMENT

In the past, most employees followed a fairly standard path of career advancement, and employers made hiring decisions accordingly. People in their twenties and thirties (the age when most started their careers) selected the path that would provide them with a fairly steady income throughout their working lives. By the time they reached their forties, these candidates had usually specialized in some aspect of their industry, so they looked for promotional advancements that rewarded them for their years of service and enabled them to continue to climb the corporate ladder. While employees in their fifties also focused on their careers, more often than not, they also found themselves balancing those professional aspirations with personal needs such as caring for children, caring for aging parents, or thinking about retirement. And if you worked into your sixties, you would look for opportunities that promised job stability until retirement.

Long-term working relationships (lasting for perhaps twenty or thirty years) were viewed as mutually beneficial, and both employers and younger job candidates seemed eager to establish them. Conversely, companies were reluctant to hire older candidates, for fear that new hires above a certain age would not be in the job long enough to justify the

**"Loyalty and enthusiasm are the two things
I value most in an employee. You're hired!"**

time and expense it would take for training and acclimation to the company culture.

In today's workplace, however, the pendulum swings in a different direction. Younger candidates are unwilling to commit to any single company for more than three to five years, while older candidates are more likely to want and need a long-term and stable working relationship.

A number of factors have contributed to this dramatic shift. In some cases, older candidates may find themselves in a situation where their investments are not doing as well as anticipated. They may face uncertainty about healthcare costs and retirement and Social Security benefits, or they may be supporting their grown children longer than anticipated, for reasons related to the economy. In addition, with people living longer today, a sixty-year-old might plan on working in her new position for another ten years, which is considerably longer than what an employer today can expect from a junior candidate. All of this bodes well for older candidates, particularly because of the loyalty factor.

Many studies have shown that the harder you work for something, the more you appreciate it. Given the additional challenges that older candidates face today as they age, they will likely appreciate the job more than their younger counterparts. Why? Because they understand how challenging it is to secure a job once you reach a certain age. From an employer's standpoint, that means an older candidate today is more likely to stay in their job rather than face the prospect of another grueling search.

> "An enthusiastic young woman came into the nursing home where I work and filled out a job application. After she left, I read her form and had to admire her honesty. To the question 'Why do you want to work here?' she had responded, 'To get experience for a better job.'"
>
> —Deborah L. Bland

The generational divide can benefit older candidates by providing them with a strategic advantage against younger candidates. Whereas a candidate in his twenties might see a position as a stepping stone for a bigger and better job a few years down the road, a candidate in her fifties can assure a prospective employer that she is not a flight risk, but rather someone who will be committed to the company for years. So, when interviewing for a position with a history of high turnover, an older candidate can present himself in a way that highlights not only his experience (and how the company will benefit from it) but also his commitment to the company if he is hired. This, in turn, provides the employer with a form of stability that will ultimately benefit the company's clients and customers.

WHAT'S GOOD FOR THE GOOSE . . .

Of course it is possible that some younger candidates are looking for a long-term working relationship and that some older candidates are not interested in working into their seventies. This just further illustrates the point that age-related decisions, regardless of whether they exclude older candidates or younger candidates, may be based on stereotypes, have no validity, and eliminate qualified candidates who might possess the precise skills the employer is eager to find.

The fact is that just as there are employers who may be reluctant to hire older applicants, there are also employers who may be reluctant to hire younger candidates.

Sloane Sippler, 38, is looking for store managers for her new group of liquor stores. She is ideally looking for people who have management experience, who will be willing to remain in a mid-level manager role, and who will understand the importance of ensuring that everyone who purchases alcohol from the store is of legal age. When reviewing the resumes to determine which applicants should move forward in the process, Sloane concludes that an older candidate would likely be the best fit for this role.

In this case, there may be just as many younger candidates who are qualified for the vacancy as older candidates. Given her predisposition, though, Sloane will likely eliminate certain applicants on the basis of age. If you are an older candidate who knows about Sloane's recruiting goals, you have a significant edge.

The point is that to climb the hill that is in front of you, you will want to not only downplay any of the negative perceptions associated with your age, but also exploit any potential positives. So, when this situation arises, take advantage of it.

> "The good thing about being old is not being young."
> STEPHEN RICHARDS

Remember, your immediate goal is not to change the world or right any wrongs, but to land a job that will give you the income you need.

Now that you are armed with this knowledge, what do you do with it? The answer to that is threefold:

1. Understand that you are looking for a job in the loyalty-free workplace, so any strategies you use will have to be responsive to today's environment.

2. Acknowledge that even though age is just a number, the way hiring managers see your age often comes down to perception.

3. Recognize that there *are* job opportunities for older candidates, but you will have to be strategic to find them.

Once you understand these dynamics, you can start to learn how to present yourself in a way that will ultimately shift the conversation to where it belongs: to your qualifications for the position and the reasons why you are the best candidate to fill the vacancy. The first step in this process is to understand that the issue is not necessarily the number on your driver's license but what the number represents. This perception, and the impact it may have on your job-search process, is precisely what we will discuss next.

Pummeling this perception, and negating the impact it may have on your job-search process, are tackled next with Strategy #1.

ABOUT THE AUTHOR

Lori B. Rassas has more than two decades of experience working on the full spectrum of employment and labor matters and more than a decade of experience teaching executives, managers, employees, and students of all levels. She received an LL.M. in Labor and Employment Law from New York University Law School, a J.D. from the George Washington University Law School, and a B.A. from Tufts University. She is also certified as a Senior Professional in Human Resources (SPHR), a trained mediator and arbitrator, and author of seven books.

Throughout her career, Lori has provided extensive workplace guidance and counsel on all phases of the employment process to both employers and employees. She has developed a pragmatic approach to the navigation of employment relationships that is derived from her experience working to resolve complex legal issues that have arisen on both sides of the bargaining table. Her prior employers include the Metropolitan Museum of Art, Columbia University, and the American Federation of Television and Radio Artists (now SAG-AFTRA), among others. She also has her own HR consulting practice, through which she offers seasoned guidance on the full scope of Human Resources matters including issues that relate to diversity and inclusion, develops and delivers training workshops, and coaches executives, managers, individual contributors, and job-seekers as to how to navigate their own workplace challenges.

Lori has taught at a number of prestigious institutions, including Columbia University's Mailman School of Public Health, Columbia University's School of Professional Studies, Fordham University School of Law, The Scheinman Institute on Conflict Resolution at Cornell University, Berkeley College, Excelsior College, and Baker College, among others.

A recognized expert on employment law and workplace issues, Lori has appeared on CNBC and has been quoted in a number of publications, including *The New York Times*, *Forbes.com*, *CNNMoney*, *Fortune*, *USA Today College*, *Women's Day*, *Aarp.org*, *nextavenue.org*, *Newsday*, *American Medical News*, and *CareerBuilder.com*.

You can connect with Lori on LinkedIn, visit her website at *www.lorirassas.com*, follow her on Twitter (@lorirassas), or connect with her consulting practice on Facebook at *www.facebook.com/loribrassas*. Lori welcomes all feedback as a way to continue to learn more about how we can make things at work work.